THE
POCKET BIBLE
SERIES

The Allotment Pocket Bible

The Baking Pocket Bible

The Camping Pocket Bible

The Cat Lover's Pocket Bible

The Christmas Pocket Bible

The Cook's Pocket Bible

The Cricket Pocket Bible

The Dad's Pocket Bible

The DIY Pocket Bible

The Dog Lover's Pocket Bible

The Football Pocket Bible

The Gardener's Pocket Bible

The Golf Pocket Bible

The Jane Austen Pocket Bible

The Knitting Pocket Bible

The Mum's Pocket Bible

The Outdoor Pocket Bible

The Pregnancy Pocket Bible

The Railway Pocket Bible

The Traveller's Pocket Bible

The Wedding Pocket Bible

The Wine Pocket Bible

THE
BAKING
POCKET BIBLE

AMY LANE

 POCKET BIBLES

This edition first published in Great Britain 2011 by
Crimson Publishing, a division of Crimson Business Ltd
Westminster House
Kew Road
Richmond
Surrey
TW9 2ND

A catalogue record for this book is available from the British Library.

ISBN 978 1 907087 127

Printed and bound by Lego Print SpA, Trento

CONTENTS

INTRODUCTION   IX

1   THE HISTORY OF BAKING   1
    Baking timeline   1
    The science of baking   3
    Baking icons   5

2   ESSENTIAL EQUIPMENT AND
    THINGS YOU NEED TO KNOW   7
    Store cupboard essentials   7
    Shorter shelf-life ingredients   8
    Basic baking equipment   9
    Desirable equipment   11
    Washing your equipment   12
    Glossary of baking terms   13
    Unusual ingredients   14
    Storage   16
    Temperature conversion chart   18
    Measurement conversion chart   19

3   CAKES   22
    Cake making methods   22
    Victoria sandwich cake   23
    Sponge cake   26
    Carrot cake   28
    Boiled fruit cake   30
    Lemon drizzle cake   32
    Farmhouse fruit cake   33

4   CUPCAKES   36
    Basic vanilla cupcake   36
    Red velvet cupcakes   39

Muffins 40
Whoopie pies 45

5 BREAD 49
Simple white loaf 50
Light wholemeal loaf 52
Soda bread 53
Brioche 55
Olive bread 57
Sundried tomato and parmesan rolls 59

6 BISCUITS AND COOKIES 61
White chocolate chip cookies 61
Ginger biscuits 63
Chocolate cream biscuits 66
Oat and sultana cookies 67
Coconut macaroons 69
Peanut butter cookies 70
Shortbread 72

7 TRADITIONAL BAKING 75
Bread pudding 75
Scones 76
Hot cross buns 79
Apple crumble 81
Pineapple upside-down pudding 82

8 COMFORT BAKING 85
Chocolate fudge cake 85
Jam roly poly 88
Apple pie 90
Flapjack 93
Swiss roll 94
Syrup sponge pudding 96

9 PASTRIES 99
Shortcrust pastry 99
Puff pastry 100
Choux pastry 100

Filo pastry 100
Cherry pie 101
Profiteroles 103
Bakewell tart 106
Plum and almond tart 108

10 CHRISTMAS BAKING 112
Mince pies 112
Homemade mincemeat 114
Christmas cake 117
Christmas pudding 120
Chocolate Yule log 122
Stollen 125

11 BAKING FOR SPECIAL OCCASIONS 128
Birthday cakes 128
Wedding cakes 130
Christening cakes 132
Easter cake 133
Halloween cakes 135

12 BAKING WITH CHILDREN 137
Gingerbread men 137
Fairy cakes 140
Smartie cookies 142
Rice Krispies cakes 144
Sugar cookies 145

13 ALLERGY-FRIENDLY BAKING 149
Flourless chocolate brownies 149
Eggless coffee cake 150
Gluten-free bread 152
Meringues 153
Dairy- and gluten-free vanilla cupcakes 155
Sugar-free ginger biscuits 157

14 DECORATION AND PRESENTATION 160
Types of icing 160
Sugar paste 163

Sugar paste decorations 167
Ideas for decorating cupcakes 168
Presentation 171

15 BAKING SOLUTIONS 173
The cake didn't rise 173
The cake rose too much 174
The pastry burnt 174
The fruit sank to the bottom 175
It's stuck to the tin 176
The cake is too dry 176
The icing is too runny 177
The bread didn't rise 177
The mixture has curdled 178
I don't have a particular ingredient 179
I don't have that piece of equipment 179

INTRODUCTION

Anyone can bake. No, really, they can. All you need are a few tried and tested recipes under your belt and before you know it, your creative streak will be running wild and beautiful home-baked goodies will be flying out of your kitchen. Soon you'll be the most popular person in your street and you'll have an exciting new hobby!

Whether you are completely new to baking or have many years' experience, *The Baking Pocket Bible* has something to offer everyone. Packed full of hints and tips, this is the book you'll turn to when you need to know what to do with your runny buttercream, how to bake the perfect scones for an afternoon tea party, what to bake for friends with special dietary requirements and when you need some inspiration for decorating your cupcakes.

For those who have mastered the art of baking, there are ideas for presenting your cakes beautifully, tips for creating sugar models and advice on how to stack a wedding cake. If you discover you have a real talent for baking and decorating cakes, then there are even some pointers on how to turn your hobby into a business.

Most importantly, you'll discover that baking is good fun and can help you relax and de-stress after a tough day. Remember, recipes are only guidelines and occasionally things may not go quite to plan but most of the time these can be salvaged – just turn to Chapter 15 for some handy tips on how to save the situation. Then dust yourself off and carry on, soon you'll know your favourite recipes off by heart. So, grab your pinny, get the children involved and get stuck in trying out some new recipes.

THE HISTORY OF BAKING

Before we get our aprons on and get started tackling some delicious recipes this chapter will take you through the history of baking, back to the earliest forms of baking, and the traditions and history that lie behind some of today's favourite baked goods.

🧁 BAKING TIMELINE 🧁

- **2500–2100BC – Evidence of bread being baked by the Egyptians.** The art of baking has been around for many thousands of years, and is thought to have originated as far back as around 2500BC in Ancient Egypt. Wall reliefs from the tomb of Rameses III show bread being baked at the royal bakery in all shapes and sizes, including in the shape of animals.

- **400BC** – Evidence of Greeks making sweetened breads and honey flans.

- **300BC – Roman bakers.** The Romans carried on the tradition of baking, often enriching their bread with eggs and butter, possibly achieving a cake-like texture. They also produced cakes which were flat and heavy, and often made from a mixture of barley, raisins, pine nuts, seeds and sweet wine. There is evidence that the Romans set up bakers' guilds from approximately 150BC.

- **AD1 – More than 300 pastry chefs in Rome.** As baking became more popular in the Roman Empire the occupation of pastry chef (or pastillarium) emerged and grew as a well-respected profession. After this, the art of baking spread throughout Europe and into parts of Asia, with early bakers' guilds evident in London and Paris in the 12th century.

- **13th century – Bread laws are introduced in England to regulate the price of bread.** During the Middle Ages, bakers started selling their produce but there was a huge amount of cheating customers out of what they had paid for, which attracted harsh penalties.

Pocket fact ━■━

To avoid being caught short-changing customers, bakers in the Middle Ages started adding an extra loaf to orders to make 13 loaves instead of 12, which became known as a baker's dozen.

- 15th century – Gingerbread becomes popular. Gingerbread merchants would sell their wares from hand carts in the streets.

- 1440s – The craft of *patissiers* is officially recognised. French and Italian chefs were credited with developing puff and choux pastries.

- 16th century – The first gingerbread man is made at the request of Queen Elizabeth I, who wanted to give some of her important visitors likenesses of themselves.

- 1800s – Bicarbonate of soda is invented, closely followed by baking powder.

- **Mid-1800s – The tradition of afternoon tea is started by Anna Russell, the seventh Duchess of Bedford**.

Afternoon tea

Who can resist the allure of tiny, perfectly cut sandwiches and dainty cakes served with pots of tea on beautiful bone china? The trend nowadays is to take afternoon tea in an expensive London hotel, some of the most famous being The Ritz, The Savoy and The Dorchester. However, the origins of afternoon tea weren't quite so lavish.

In the mid-1800s it was fashionable to just have two main meals a day; breakfast in the morning and dinner at around 8 o'clock in the evening. A light meal, known as luncheon was then introduced, but some people, such as Anna Russell, the seventh Duchess of Bedford, complained that by about 4 o'clock in the afternoon they were hungry. So the Duchess started having a pot of tea and a snack of sandwiches and cake brought to her in her room in Woburn Abbey during the afternoon. Soon she began to invite friends along to share 'afternoon tea' with her and so the tradition began.

The afternoon tea that is served nowadays usually consists of sandwiches, often filled with smoked salmon, egg and thinly sliced cucumber, scones served with clotted cream and jam, and an assortment of delicate cakes and pastries.

- 1861 – Mrs Beeton publishes her *Book of Household Management*, which later led to many recipe books being written.

- 1890s – The first electric ovens become available.

- 1929 – Scientists report the benefits of wholemeal flour.

- 1930 – Wonderbread produces the first sliced bread in Britain.

- 1950 – Invention and launch in the UK of the Kenwood Chef food mixer, making home baking a much easier task.

- 2000s – The rise of the cupcakery: the technique spreads from the USA to the UK.

🧁 THE SCIENCE OF BAKING 🧁

Without the modern equipment that is available today, cake making often seemed to be a laborious and time-consuming task. To begin with, yeast was usually the main leavening ingredient. When yeast is mixed with sugar and flour and left in a warm place it produces bubbles of carbon dioxide and makes bread and cakes rise.

In the early 18th century, people began making cakes without yeast though, meaning that the best way to make sure the cake would rise was to beat the eggs well to incorporate lots of air. Some recipes even called for as many as 30 eggs and required them to be beaten for several hours!

Pocket fact -■-

Chaucer wrote of cakes in the 14th century, referring to one as containing 13kg of flour alone as well as butter, cream, eggs, spices, currants and honey.

In the early 1800s bicarbonate of soda (known as baking soda in the USA) was discovered and began to change the way cakes were baked. Bicarbonate of soda is an alkaline substance, and when it's mixed with an acid, such as buttermilk, lemon juice, vinegar or cream of tartar, it reacts to form tiny air bubbles of carbon dioxide in the mixture. Soon after this, baking powder, a mix of bicarbonate of soda and either cream of tartar or tartaric acid, was introduced, making baking even easier.

Pocket tip 🍪

Raising agents, such as baking powder and bicarbonate of soda, have a limited life once opened. You can test if they will still work by dropping a teaspoon of it into a cup of water and watching to see if the water fizzes. If it does, then the baking powder or soda is still active.

Five firsts

- *The first wedding cakes were known as 'bride cakes' or 'great cakes'. They weren't called wedding cakes until the 19th century.*
- *The first author to write about a fruit cake decorated with marzipan and royal icing was Elizabeth Raffald in 1769.*

- *Although cakes have been eaten for centuries to celebrate different occasions, the first birthday cakes, as we know them today, emerged in the mid-19th century.*
- *Cupcakes were first mentioned in Eliza Leslie's cookbook* Receipts *in 1828.*
- *London's first cupcakery was the Buttercup cake shop, which opened in 2007.*

Pocket fact ■

There are two theories about where the name cupcakes come from. The first is that they were usually baked in individual pottery cups or moulds and the second is because a cupful of each of the ingredients was used in the mixture.

🧁 BAKING ICONS 🧁

Over the years, as baking became a commonplace activity in many homes some baking stars began to emerge – talented bakers who produced books and television programmes to guide budding bakers. Here we look at just a few of these baking icons.

Mrs Beeton

Isabella Mary Beeton, known as Mrs Beeton, was born in 1836 and died at the age of just 28. She is one of the most famous cookery writers in British history and was the author of *Mrs Beeton's Book of Household Management*, the forerunner to many cookery and baking books.

Mary Berry

Mary Berry is a famous cookery writer who started out as a cookery magazine editor. She is especially well known for her baking skills and for writing about AGA cookery. Mary makes regular TV and radio appearances in the UK and has written over 70 best-selling cookery books.

Jane Asher

Although she is a well-known actress, Jane Asher also forged a second career for herself as a cake decorator. She has written several books on cake decorating and runs her own cake business, Jane Asher Party Cakes and Sugarcraft, in London.

Nigella Lawson

Nigella Lawson is a famous food writer and TV presenter. In 2000 she wrote a book entitled *How to be a Domestic Goddess*, which had a large focus on baking and led to her first TV series *Nigella Bites*. Since then she has written many more cookery books and presented more TV series, including the popular *Nigella's Christmas Kitchen*.

Paul Hollywood

Paul Hollywood is one of the UK's leading artisan bakers and has also enjoyed a successful career as a best-selling author and TV chef. He has worked in many top hotels both in the UK and abroad, and in 2010 was one of the judges in the popular TV show *The Great British Bake Off*.

Pocket fact ‑■‑

Cake moulds have been used since the mid-17th century. Early moulds would have been wooden hoops placed on a baking tray.

2

ESSENTIAL EQUIPMENT AND THINGS YOU NEED TO KNOW

The beauty of baking is that you don't need to invest in a lot of expensive equipment. With a few basic pieces of equipment, a well-stocked store cupboard and some knowledge of a few common baking terms, you can make a whole host of wonderful creations in your home kitchen.

🧁 STORE CUPBOARD ESSENTIALS 🧁

There are a few basic ingredients that are always useful to keep stocked up on, many of which have a long shelf life. This means that as long as they are stored correctly, they will keep well. Some ingredients have a shorter shelf-life so they need to be bought when you are planning to bake.

It's a good idea to keep your cupboard and fridge stocked with these basics:

- Self-raising flour
- Plain flour
- Baking powder
- Bicarbonate of soda
- Cocoa powder
- Caster sugar
- Icing sugar
- Golden syrup

- Vanilla extract

- Selection of dried fruit

- Selection of spices – eg ground ginger, cinnamon, mixed spice, nutmeg

Pocket tip 🍪

Keep an eye on the use-by date for your herbs and spices — they can usually be stored in glass jars in a cool, dark place for up to a year. Whole (unground) spices will last longer than this.

🧁 SHORTER SHELF-LIFE 🧁 INGREDIENTS

These are the items you may need occasionally for your baking but will need to buy just before you plan to bake as they have a shorter shelf-life.

- Butter

- Buttermilk (see p. 179 for how to make a buttermilk substitute)

- Cream

- Eggs

- Crème fraiche

- Sour cream

- Milk

- Natural yoghurt

- Cream cheese

Five handy cake-decorating edibles

Keep a few cake-decorating items in the house for those last minute rushes. These will all keep well if stored in a cool dry place. Keep any open packets of edibles that can't easily be resealed wrapped in clingfilm or stored in an airtight container.

- *A selection of gel food colours*
- *Edible glue*
- *Sugar paste (see p. 163)*
- *Small selection of cake decorations and sprinkles*
- *Marzipan*

🧁 BASIC BAKING EQUIPMENT 🧁

With such a huge choice of tempting bakeware available in the shops and on the internet, it's difficult not to get carried away! There are a few essentials that you need to get you started, and the rest you can build up as and when you need it.

Pocket tip 🎅

Remember that baking tins are bulky to store so check you've got room before your collection gets too large!

Essential baking equipment

- 2 × 7 inch (18cm) sandwich tins
- 8 inch (20cm) square baking tin
- 8 inch (20cm) round baking tin
- 2lb loaf tin

Pocket tip 🎅

Always try to buy non-stick bakeware and wash it by hand — not in the dishwasher!

- Sieve
- Measuring jug

- Measuring spoons
- Accurate weighing scales (electronic are usually best)
- Flexible scraper spatula
- Large mixing bowl
- Selection of smaller bowls
- Large rolling pin (non-stick is best)
- Balloon whisk
- Electric hand whisk
- Sharp knives
- Greaseproof paper
- Pastry brush (silicone is best)
- Skewers
- Cake storage tins or airtight containers
- Baking beans
- Baking trays
- Cookie cutter
- Muffin tin
- Wooden spoon
- Cupcake cases

Pocket tip 🕴

If you need a particular type of baking tin for a one-off use, you can often hire them for a small charge from your local cake-decorating shop, or sometimes from an online supplier.

Five useful online suppliers

Sometimes you need to buy something a bit unusual or perhaps buy in bulk and this can often be easier, and cheaper, to do online. Here are some useful cake supplies websites:

- *www.cakecraftshop.co.uk*
- *www.windsorcakecraft.co.uk*
- *www.squires-shop.com*
- *www.cakestinsandfavours.co.uk*
- *www.cakescookiesandcraftsshop.co.uk*

🧁 DESIRABLE EQUIPMENT 🧁

Of course, there are some items that aren't absolutely necessary but can make your life a whole lot easier when you are baking. Here are a few things that you might like to add to your birthday list!

- **Electric food mixer, such as a Kenwood Chef or KitchenAid**. Food mixers come with lots of attachments often including a whisk, beater, dough hook and food processor attachment. A very handy piece of kit and great for those who are short of time in the kitchen but love to bake.

- **Bread machine**. It's always wonderful to come down in the morning to the smell of freshly baked bread and you can do just that with a bread machine. You simply place all the ingredients in and let the machine do the hard work for you. Many machines also have the function to make cakes and jam.

- **Oven thermometer**. It's very useful to have an oven thermometer. It isn't uncommon for the actual temperature of the oven to be quite different from what you think you've set it at! An oven thermometer will help you find the right temperature and make it easier for you when you are trying out new recipes.

- **Cake-decorating equipment**. This includes a sugar shaper, veining tool, ball tool, petal pad and ribbon cutters.

Five handy pieces of cake-decorating equipment

Unless you are planning on starting your own baking business, you don't need to invest heavily in lots of cake-decorating equipment, but there are some useful items you may want to consider buying.

- *Some basic piping nozzles – a small star tip, large star tip, and a small round one for writing are very useful.*
- *Cupcake/muffin cases – standard size and mini-muffin cases are often available.*
- *Sugar and flour shakers – make sure you label which is which!*
- *Small non-stick rolling pin – great for rolling out sugar paste.*
- *Cake smoothers – to smooth out the lumps and bumps when you cover a cake in sugar paste to give a neat finish.*

🧁 WASHING YOUR EQUIPMENT 🧁

All equipment should be kept clean and ideally washed in hot soapy water before and after use. Any equipment that is dishwasher safe should be washed regularly in a dishwasher as the high temperatures help to kill bacteria. Think carefully about how you store your equipment, both to make sure it stays in good working order and to keep it hygienic.

Change dishcloths, tea towels and hand towels regularly in the kitchen and wash them on a high heat. Make sure there is kitchen roll available for drying hands and mopping up spills. Use an anti-bacterial spray on all work surfaces and tiles before and after you bake.

Pocket tip 🍪

If you are baking commercially it's recommended that you dry your hands on disposable paper towels each time you wash them.

🧁 GLOSSARY OF BAKING TERMS 🧁

Here are a few specific baking terms which you might come across.

- **Bain marie**. This is a French term which means 'water bath'. When cooking items such as cheesecakes or custard-based desserts in the oven they may be placed in a tray of water, which helps to regulate the temperature and provide moisture. Chocolate may be melted in a *bain marie* – this usually means a bowl placed over the top of a saucepan containing simmering water.

- **Beat**. This means to stir vigorously, often with a wooden spoon. You can also beat cake batters using a food mixer with a beater blade.

- **Blind bake**. This is the act of baking pastry before the filling is added to make sure the pastry is cooked through. A pastry case is usually pricked with a fork, lined with greaseproof paper and filled with baking beans or rice and then baked.

- **Cream together**. This is most commonly used at the beginning of cake recipes to describe the method of combining the fat and sugar. You can use a wooden spoon or food mixer to do this and should beat the mixture until it's light and fluffy and no lumps of butter are visible.

- **Fold**. This usually describes how you mix in an ingredient, such as flour, whisked egg whites or ground almonds. It's most common to use a metal spoon to do this as it cuts cleanly through the cake batter without knocking out the air.

- **Knead**. This term is usually used in breadmaking to describe the action of working the dough with your hands. Press the dough away from you with the heel of your hand, fold it back towards yourself, then give it a quarter turn – repeat until the dough is smooth and stretchy. You will need to do this for approximately 8–10 minutes by hand or 5–7 minutes if you are using a food mixer with a dough hook attachment.

- **Rub in**. A method of combining the fat and flour, often using the fingertips to rub the ingredients together to make a breadcrumb-like texture. You can also use a pastry blender or food processor to achieve the same effect.

- **Separating eggs**. This is when you separate the egg yolks from the eggs whites. You can do this in several ways including cracking the shell gently to trap the yolk but letting the white through or you can buy a special gadget that will hold the yolk and let the white through. You can even use your hand to hold the yolk but let the white run through your fingertips.

- **Whisk**. Using either a hand or electric whisk to beat, often eggs, to add air and give volume to the mixture.

🧁 UNUSUAL INGREDIENTS 🧁

Sometimes a recipe calls for a slightly more unusual ingredient that you wouldn't normally keep in your store cupboard. Luckily though, many of these ingredients are now available in the baking section of supermarkets. If you can't find it there, try a health food shop as these shops often stock unusual ingredients and also product substitutes for those with allergies to regular baking ingredients.

- **Agar agar**. A gelatine substitute suitable for vegetarians that is made from seaweed. It is available in flake and powder form and is used for thickening sauces.

- **Arrowroot**. A thickener, which is especially useful for thickening acidic sauces and fruit gels to go over flans.

- **Carob**. A chocolate substitute made from the ground pods of the carob tree. It's usually available as a powder, a bar or as carob chips and is often used in vegan recipes.

- **Cream of tartar**. A by-product of winemaking. It's often used to stabilise egg whites and help create volume when the whites are being whisked, and is usually one of the components, along with bicarbonate of soda, in baking powder.

- **Dried egg albumen**. This comes in powder form and is dried pasteurised egg albumen (egg white). Because of the pasteurisation process, there is no risk of contracting salmonella.

The powder needs to be reconstituted wih water before use. It is available in some supermarkets or from cake decorating supply shops.

- **Gelatine**. A setting agent that can be bought in powder or leaf form; it's unsuitable for vegetarians as it is an animal by-product.

- **Glycerine**. A thick, clear liquid with a slightly sweet taste. It's often used to soften royal icing.

- **Gum tragacanth**. This is usually available in powder form and is most likely to be found in cake decorating shops or online. It comes from the dried sap of Middle Eastern legumes and is added to sugar paste to make it easier to roll thin and so that it sets hard.

- **Liquid glucose**. A thick, clear, sweet syrup that helps control the formation of sugar crystals. Especially useful when making frozen desserts, ice creams, confectionery and jams.

- **Sugar syrup**. This is a liquid used for sweetening and is also great for brushing onto cakes to keep them moist. You can make your own by bringing 75g caster sugar and 75ml of water to the boil in a small saucepan. Stir to dissolve then set aside to cool.

- **Vegetable fat**. A solid white vegetable fat, known as shortening in the US, often used in pastry making. Common UK brands are Trex, Cookeen and White Flora.

Food safety tips

It's important to maintain good food hygiene and safety practices when you are baking. In particular, make sure you store baking ingredients away from raw meat in the fridge, always wash your hands before and after baking and keep all equipment clean and stored safely.

Pocket tip 🍪

If you are planning on turning your home baking hobby into a business, make sure you follow the guidelines set out by your local council. You usually need to register as a food business at least 28 days before trading, obtain a food hygiene certificate and have your kitchen inspected by your local environmental health team.

🧁 STORAGE 🧁

It's always a good idea to check the packaging for your baking ingredients as it will usually give you a good idea of how they are best stored.

Dry ingredients such as flour and sugar are best stored in airtight containers. Self-raising flour has added raising agents, which will begin to lose their effectiveness once opened, so make sure you take a note of the best-before date and when you opened the flour. The same happens with baking powder and bicarbonate of soda.

Butter should be stored in the fridge and in most cases should be removed a few hours before you are going to use it so it can come to room temperature.

Pocket tip 🍪

Always keep an eye on the best-before dates, especially for ingredients you may not use often, such as shop-bought cake decorations.

STORING YOUR BAKED GOODS

It is best to store your baked goods in an airtight container and unless your recipe includes fresh cream or cream cheese frosting, you do not need to store them in the fridge.

As a guide:

- Larger cakes and cupcakes will last for about three days.

- Bread will stay fresh for two days when kept in an airtight container or bread bag.

- Biscuits and cookies will keep for two to three days.

- Cakes that have been covered in fondant will last longer, especially if they have been brushed with sugar syrup (see unusual ingredients list), and will keep uncut for a week. Once cut they will keep fresh for around three days.

- Fruit cakes last a long time and are better when matured for at least three months. They should be wrapped in greaseproof paper and foil, and stored in a cool dry place. Once cut they will keep for a week or more.

EGGS

The current recommendation is that eggs should ideally be stored in the fridge, away from other foods. Always check the shell isn't damaged before you use an egg and that they haven't reached their use-by date.

It's important to handle eggs carefully to avoid any contamination and the risk of salmonella infection. Bacteria can be present on the outside of the shell as well as the inside, so always wash your hands well after handling eggs.

Always make sure eggs are properly cooked when you are catering for the very young, elderly, pregnant women or those who are unwell as they are more at risk of becoming ill.

Top tips when using eggs

- *To test if an egg is fresh place it in a bowl of water. If it sinks to the bottom it is fresh. If it floats it is past its best and has most likely gone bad. If it partially floats with its broader end towards the surface then it is an older egg, but is still fine to use.*

- *Always break eggs into a small bowl one at a time before adding them to your recipe. This means you can double check they are fresh and remove any pieces of shell that might get in.*
- *Use the empty half of an egg shell to remove any pieces that fall in when you crack your egg open – they seem to attract each other and are easily removed.*

🧁 TEMPERATURE CONVERSION 🧁 CHART

As mentioned earlier, it's a good idea to test your oven with an oven thermometer to get an idea of how the actual temperature compares with what the dial says. Remember if you have a fan oven you will probably need to lower the temperature by about 10°C. Here is a handy guide to converting temperatures.

Celsius (°C)	Fahrenheit (°F)	Gas mark
130°C	250°F	½
140°C	275°F	1
150°C	300°F	2
160°C	320°F	2
170°C	325°F	3
180°C	350°F	4
190°C	375°F	5
200°C	400°F	6
220°C	425°F	7

Pocket tip 🍪

If you find your baking is taking longer than the recipe states then try baking it for longer, checking every 5 minutes, moving it to a higher shelf or maybe turning your oven up a little higher next time.

Common baking abbreviations

Most baking recipes will include a whole host of abbreviations, especially for different measurements. Here are some of the most common ones you will encounter:

- **tsp**. *Teaspoon, equivalent to 5ml*
- **tbsp**. *Tablespoon, equivalent to 15ml*
- **g**. *Grams, there are 1,000g in a kg*
- **kg**. *Kilograms*
- **ml**. *Millilitres, there are 1,000ml in a litre*
- **lb**. *Pounds*
- **oz**. *Ounces, there are 16oz in a lb*

Pocket fact ▬

There are approximately 25g in 1oz.

🧁 MEASUREMENT CONVERSION 🧁 CHART

Most UK recipes are now written in metric units but some recipes passed down through families or in older recipes books may be written using imperial measurements. There are also a lot of popular recipes available from the USA now, which are often written using cups as measures. Here are a few guidelines for converting measurements.

CONVERTING WEIGHTS

Ounces and pounds	Grams
1/4oz	5g
1/2oz	10g
1oz	25g
4oz	110g
8oz	225g
1lb	450g
2lb	900g

CONVERTING VOLUMES

Pints	Millilitres	Cups (USA)
1/4pt	150ml	1/2 cup
1/2pt	275ml	1 cup
3/4pt	425ml	1 1/2 cups
1pt	570ml	2 cups

SPOONS

Spoon	Millilitres
1 teaspoon	5ml
1 dessertspoon	10ml
1 tablespoon	15ml

Pocket tip 🍪

When following a recipe stick to either metric or imperial measurements, never mix the two.

The conversion tables in this chapter are intended as a guide but are only approximations which have been rounded up or down. Due to the variations between the metric and imperial systems you may find slightly different conversions in different sources. You should always use the amount which suits your own personal preference.

3

CAKES

Cake mixture recipes are the bedrock of baking. Knowing how to make a good cake, and then discovering the endless number of varieties you can produce makes cake baking a joyful task and an integral part of the baking experience.

🧁 CAKE MAKING METHODS 🧁

When it comes to making cakes there are four main methods.

THE WHISKING METHOD

This is when eggs and sugar are whisked together to incorporate air, and then the flour is folded in afterwards. As the cake cooks, the little bubbles of air expand, which causes the cake to rise. This creates a texture of tiny holes in the cake, resembling a sponge, and is why this method produces a cake known as sponge cake.

Pocket tip

Folding the flour in using a metal spoon means it cuts more cleanly through the cake batter and less air is knocked out of the mixture.

THE CREAMING METHOD

The fat and sugar are creamed together first before adding the beaten eggs and flour. This produces a slightly firmer texture than the whisking method and is used for cakes such as a Victoria sandwich.

THE RUBBING-IN METHOD

First the fat and flour are rubbed together, then the other ingredients are mixed in. This usually produces a crumblier, drier texture, such as in rock cakes or scones.

Pocket tip 🧍

Always make sure you have cool, dry hands when you are rubbing fat and flour together as this makes the fat less likely to melt quickly and stick to your fingers.

THE MELTING METHOD

This is also sometimes known as the muffin method in the USA. The fat and sugar are melted together first. This method produces a denser cake, such as gingerbread.

THE 'ALL-IN-ONE' METHOD

With so much new technology around nowadays, it's also easy to make a cake using the 'all-in-one' method. This does exactly what it says on the tin – put all the ingredients together into an electric food mixer and mix. Just be careful not to over-mix them!

Pocket tip 🧍

Always make sure all your ingredients are at room temperature before you start baking. This means they will combine more easily and give your cake an even texture.

🧁 VICTORIA SANDWICH CAKE 🧁

This old favourite is named after Queen Victoria and is made using the creaming method. Traditionally, the cake is split into two, filled with jam and dusted with icing sugar, although nowadays it's also often filled with buttercream or cream and is often iced as well. To save you having to split the cake, you can bake it in two sandwich tins.

Pocket fact ■

This cake is often referred to, wrongly, as a Victoria sponge cake. It is actually not a sponge cake because it is made using the creaming method, not the whisking method.

Ingredients

(Serves 12)

- 175g butter or baking margarine, softened
- 175g caster sugar
- 175g self-raising flour
- 3 eggs
- 1tsp vanilla extract

Pocket tip 🍪

To soften your butter either leave it out of the fridge for a few hours or warm it in the microwave on a medium heat for 10 seconds at a time until it's soft.

Method

1. Preheat your oven to 180°C (350°F or gas mark 4). Grease and line 2 round 7 inch (18cm) sandwich tins.

2. Cream together the butter and sugar in a large bowl using a wooden spoon. You can also do this in a food mixer on a slow speed.

3. In a jug, whisk together the eggs and vanilla extract.

4. When the butter and sugar are well combined and look pale and fluffy, begin to add the egg mix a little at a time.

Pocket tip 🕴

Add a spoonful of flour each time you add some egg — this will help stop the mixture curdling.

5. Once all of the egg has been added, fold in the remaining flour with a metal spoon.

6. Divide the mixture equally between the 2 sandwich tins and level the surface with a spatula or the back of a spoon.

Pocket tip 🕴

Making a slight hollow in the centre of the mixture with a spoon will help the cake to rise more evenly, without a domed top.

7. Bake for 25–30 minutes until the cakes are risen and golden and the cake springs back when gently pressed.

8. Leave to cool in the tins for 5 minutes then turn out onto a wire rack and leave to cool completely.

9. Fill with your favourite jam and dust with icing sugar.

Pocket tip 🕴

A Victoria sandwich will keep in a cake tin for several days. You can also freeze this type of cake so you'll always have something handy to offer guests!

Variations to try

● *To make a light chocolate cake replace 25g of the self-raising flour with cocoa powder and add 1tsp baking powder and 1tbsp milk.*

- *For a delicious coffee cake, dissolve 1tbsp of instant coffee in 1tbsp of boiling water and add to the cake mixture.*
- *To give the cake a zesty kick, add 1tbsp of lemon curd and the finely grated zest of 1 lemon to the cake batter.*

🧁 SPONGE CAKE 🧁

There are two methods for making a sponge cake, the Genoese (or Genoise) and the Savoy.

The Genoese method involves whisking whole eggs with the sugar before folding in the flour. The Savoy method requires the eggs to be separated first (see p. 14 for tips on how to separate eggs). The yolks are then beaten with the sugar and the flour folded in, followed by whisked egg whites.

The Genoese method is more commonly used and is ideal for making Swiss rolls, sponge fingers and madeleines. Sponge cakes can also be split and filled, or baked in two separate tins and filled, or eaten plain.

GENOESE SPONGE CAKE

Ingredients

(Serves 10)

- 3 eggs
- 75g caster sugar
- 75g self-raising flour
- $^{1}/_{2}$tsp vanilla extract

Pocket tip 🧍

It is best to use a good-quality vanilla extract, usually labelled as 'pure' or 'natural' vanilla extract, when baking. You will need to use much less if you use good quality stuff and the flavour is much better. Cheap vanilla essence is only flavouring that doesn't actually come from the vanilla pod.

Method

1. Preheat the oven to 190°C (375°F or gas mark 5). Grease 2 round 7 inch (18cm) sandwich tins, sprinkle some flour into them. Shake the tins to coat the bottom and sides with the flour.

2. Whisk together the eggs, sugar and vanilla extract in a large bowl. It is best to do this with an electric hand whisk or a food mixer with a whisk attachment. You are aiming to get as much air incorporated as you can or the cakes won't rise.

Pocket tip ♟

To test if you have whisked enough the mixture should become very pale and when you lift out the whisk, the drops should form ribbons which stay on the surface of the mix for a few seconds before vanishing.

3. Sift the flour and fold it in carefully using a metal spoon.

4. Pour into the prepared tins, tilting them to make sure the mixture is evenly distributed.

5. Bake in the centre of the oven for around 20 minutes until the cakes are golden and the top springs back when you press it gently.

Pocket tip ♟

Never open the oven door early on in the baking process. The rush of cold will stop the air bubbles in the cake expanding and can actually cause them to contract instead, making your cake sink instead of rise.

6. Leave the cakes to cool in the tins for a few minutes before turning them out onto a wire rack to cool completely.

7. Spread the cakes with a filling of your choice (see p. 160), dust with icing sugar and serve.

Because there is very little fat in a sponge cake they don't last long and are best eaten on the day they are made.

> ## Variations to try
> - *To make a chocolate Genoese cake, sift 1tbsp of cocoa powder in with the flour.*
> - *You can experiment with various fillings such as different jams, buttercream (see recipe on p. 160), whipped cream and fresh fruit, lemon curd and chocolate ganache.*

🧁 CARROT CAKE 🧁

Carrots are a naturally sweet vegetable, containing more sugar than most other vegetables. This means they work well in cakes and baking. They have been used in baking since the medieval period but carrot cake became popular again during the Second World War because of rationing. Carrots were much more widely available than sugar and had the advantage that they could be grown at home. Carrot cake is now a regular on café menus and is particularly popular in the USA, where it is often served with cream cheese frosting. The carrots help add moisture to the cake and give it a dense texture.

Ingredients

(Serves 12)

- 200g plain flour
- 1tsp ground cinnamon
- 2tsp baking powder
- 150g light muscovado sugar
- 3 eggs
- 200ml vegetable oil
- 200g carrots, grated
- 50g walnuts, coarsely chopped

Method

1. Preheat the oven to 180°C (350°F or gas mark 4). Grease and line a round 7 inch (18cm) cake tin.

2. Sieve the flour, cinnamon and baking powder into a large mixing bowl then add the sugar.

Pocket tip 🍪

Holding the sieve up high above the bowl as you sieve the flour will help get air into the mixture.

3. In a separate jug, lightly whisk together the eggs and vegetable oil.

4. Gradually pour the egg and oil mixture into the flour, stirring with a wooden spoon all the time. You could use a food mixer to do this if you have one.

5. Add the grated carrots and walnuts and mix to combine.

6. Pour into the prepared tin and level the surface.

7. Bake for around 35–40 minutes until the cake is risen and golden.

Pocket tip 🍪

You can check if your cake is cooked by inserting a metal skewer or small knife into the centre of the cake. If it comes out clean then the cake is cooked through.

8. Leave the cake to cool in the tin for 10 minutes, then turn out onto a wire rack to cool completely.

9. Decorate with cream cheese icing (see below), or simply mix some sifted icing sugar with a few drops of water to make an icing.

> ## Variations to try
> - *Try adding chopped hazelnuts instead of the walnuts, or a couple of tablespoons of sultanas.*

CREAM CHEESE ICING

This icing is a great alternative to buttercream and isn't quite so sweet. It works well as both a topping and a filling for a cake. It can be piped or spread on cupcakes too.

Ingredients

(Makes enough to ice the top of 1 cake or 24 cupcakes)

- 125g butter, softened
- 200g cream cheese, room temperature
- 400g icing sugar
- ½tsp vanilla extract

Method

1. Beat together the butter and cream cheese until they are well combined and there are no lumps. It is easiest to do this in a food mixer or with an electric hand whisk.

2. Add the vanilla extract and sift in half the icing sugar. Beat until combined.

3. Add the rest of the icing sugar and beat again until it's all incorporated.

4. Spread or pipe onto your chosen cake or cupcakes.

🧁 BOILED FRUIT CAKE 🧁

This is a deliciously moist fruit cake that is very simple to bake. You can use any combination of dried fruit such as currants, raisins, sultanas, cherries, mixed peel, dates, apricots, or buy a bag of mixed dried fruit. There are some great bags of mixed dried fruit in the supermarkets, even some luxury ones, which contain more exotic fruits, such as pineapple.

Pocket tip 🧑

Always wash your dried fruit thoroughly under cold running water before starting your recipe and leave it to drain. This removes any impurities.

Ingredients

(Makes 15 slices)

- 225g butter
- 350g dried mixed fruit
- 125g light muscovado sugar
- 285ml milk
- 3 eggs
- 275g self-raising flour

Method

1. Preheat the oven to 150°C (300°F or gas mark 2). Grease and line a 2lb loaf tin.

2. Place the butter, sugar, dried fruit and milk in a saucepan and bring to the boil. Simmer for 10 minutes.

3. Remove the pan from the heat and allow to cool.

4. Beat the eggs in a measuring jug then stir them into the fruit mixture.

5. Fold in the flour using a wooden spoon until it's all incorporated and pour the mixture into the prepared loaf tin.

6. Bake for $1^{1}/4$ to $1^{1}/2$ hours until a skewer inserted into the cake comes out clean.

7. Allow to cool in the tin for half an hour then turn out onto a wire rack to cool completely.

Pocket fact ▬

Boiling the fruit in liquid helps to partially rehydrate it, adding more moisture to the cake.

Variations to try

- *Experiment with different types of dried fruit or try adding a handful of chopped walnuts for a nutty texture.*
- *To make this into a lovely fruity tea loaf, replace the milk with freshly brewed black tea. This cake will keep well in a cake tin for several days.*

🧁 LEMON DRIZZLE CAKE 🧁

This zingy lemon cake is always a big hit at tea time and is guaranteed to become a family favourite. Using granulated sugar for the lemon drizzle topping creates a lovely crunchy topping to the cake, while the syrup sinks in making the cake wonderfully moist.

Pocket tip 🍪

If you are serving your cake on a plate, lightly dust the plate with icing sugar to prevent the cake from sticking to the plate.

Ingredients

(Serves 12)

- 200g caster sugar
- 200g butter, softened
- 3 eggs
- 200g self-raising flour
- Zest of 1 lemon, finely grated

For the drizzle topping

- Juice of 1 lemon
- 50g granulated sugar

Method

1. Preheat the oven to 170°C (325°F or gas mark 3). Grease and line a 2lb loaf tin.

2. Cream together the softened butter and sugar in a large bowl, or use a food mixer.

3. Whisk the eggs in a jug, then gradually add them to the mixture. Add a spoonful of flour each time you add the eggs to stop the mixture from curdling.

4. Sift in the remaining flour and fold it in with a wooden spoon, then stir in the finely grated lemon zest.

5. Pour the mixture into the prepared tin and bake for 40–45 minutes until the cake is golden and a skewer inserted into the centre of the cake comes out clean.

6. While the cake cools in the tin for 5 minutes, mix the lemon juice and granulated sugar together in a small bowl until they are combined, but the sugar hasn't dissolved.

7. Prick the cake all over with the skewer – this helps the cake to absorb some of the lemon drizzle syrup, making it lovely and moist.

8. Spoon the drizzle syrup slowly over the cake, then leave to cool in the tin.

9. Turn out and serve.

Variations to try

- *To make a zesty St Clements drizzle cake, add the zest of an orange to the cake mix and the juice of the orange to the drizzle topping.*
- *For a delicious lemon and poppy seed cake, add 2tbsp of poppy seeds to the cake mixture before pouring into the cake tin.*

🧁 FARMHOUSE FRUIT CAKE 🧁

This is a light fruit cake, somewhere between a plain Victoria sandwich and a fruit cake, and is an ideal lighter alternative to a heavy fruit cake. It is perfect for lazy Sunday afternoon teas or lunchboxes.

Ingredients

(Serves 12)

- 175g butter or baking margarine, softened
- 175g caster sugar
- 3 eggs
- 3tbsp milk
- 350g self-raising flour
- 1tsp mixed spice
- 85g sultanas
- 85g raisins
- 85g glacé cherries, quartered

Method

1. Preheat the oven to 170°C (325°F or gas mark 3). Grease and line an 8 inch (20cm) round cake tin.

2. Place the butter, sugar, milk, eggs, flour and mixed spice in a large mixing bowl and mix until combined and smooth – a food mixer is ideal if you have one.

3. Wash the dried fruit and, along with the glacé cherries, stir it into the cake batter.

Pocket tip 🧍

Toss the cherries in a little flour before adding them to the mixture. This stops them from sinking to the bottom of the cake.

4. Put the cake mixture into the prepared tin and smooth the top with a spatula or the back of a spoon. Make a slight hollow in the centre of the top to help the cake rise more evenly.

5. Place in the centre of the oven and bake for about 1^1/2 hours until it's golden and a skewer inserted into the centre comes out clean.

6. Leave to cool in the tin for 5 minutes then turn out onto a wire rack to cool completely.

Pocket tip 🍪

If the top of your cake starts to become too brown when you are baking a fruit cake, place a circle of baking paper on the top to stop it getting burnt.

Variation to try

- *As a slight variation, to make a cherry cake, replace the sultanas and raisins with chopped glacé cherries.*

4

CUPCAKES

Over the past few years cupcakes have become extremely popular, with cupcake shops springing up on many street corners and couples often opting for large cupcake towers as their wedding cake. Cupcakes are often described as a little bite of heaven, a perfectly sized cake that you can have all to yourself, and are often characterised by a large swirl of buttercream frosting piped high on the top. Once you have perfected a basic cupcake recipe you can try out many different flavour and topping combinations to wow your friends and family.

🧁 BASIC VANILLA CUPCAKE 🧁

This is a simple cupcake recipe, which once perfected, you can add to and adapt to create many different flavours.

Ingredients

(Makes 12)

- 125g butter, softened
- 125g caster sugar
- 125g self-raising flour
- 1tsp baking powder
- 2 eggs
- 1tsp vanilla extract

Method

1. Preheat the oven to 170°C (325°F or gas mark 3) and place 12 cupcake cases in the wells of a 12-hole muffin tin.

2. Cream together the butter and sugar with a wooden spoon in a large bowl until it is light and fluffy. You can also use a food mixer to do this.

3. Whisk together the eggs and vanilla in a jug.

4. Sift together the flour and baking powder.

Pocket tip 🍪

If you don't have a sieve you can mix the flour and baking powder using a whisk, as this will add the same amount of air to the mixture.

5. Gradually add the eggs to the butter and sugar mix, adding a tablespoon of flour each time you add some egg to prevent the mixture from curdling.

6. Once all of the egg has been added, fold in the remaining flour with a metal spoon.

7. Divide the mixture equally between the 12 cupcake cases.

Pocket tip 🍪

Using a medium-sized spring-loaded scoop can help put equal amounts of cake batter into each case.

8. Bake for 15–20 minutes until the cupcakes are risen and golden, and spring back when the centre is pressed lightly.

Pocket tip 🍪

If you want lovely flat tops to your cupcakes to help with decoration then don't overfill the cases and experiment with turning your oven down to a slightly lower temperature.

9. Leave the cupcakes to cool in the tin for 5 minutes then remove them and leave to cool on a wire rack.

10. When they are completely cool you can decorate them with buttercream, glacé icing or just enjoy them plain.

Variations to try

- For delicious chocolate cupcakes replace 25g of the self-raising flour with 25g of cocoa powder and add $^{1}/_{2}$tsp more baking powder. Decorate with chocolate buttercream or dark chocolate ganache.

- Turn your basic cupcakes into lovely coffee cupcakes by mixing 2tsp of instant coffee granules with 2tsp of boiling water and adding to the cake batter. Ice with coffee buttercream and decorate with half a walnut.

- To make light lemon and poppy seed cupcakes add the finely grated zest of one lemon, 1 dessertspoon of lemon curd and 1tbsp of poppy seeds to the basic cupcake recipe. To decorate mix 50g icing sugar with enough lemon juice to make a pouring consistency and drizzle over the cupcakes.

Pocket fact ━■━

There have been many attempts at baking the world's largest cupcake. The latest record-breaking cupcake was baked in Detroit, Michigan, USA, and was made from 200lb (about 91kg) of flour, 200lb (about 91kg) of sugar, 200lb (about 91kg) of butter and 800 eggs. It was baked for over 12 hours and had a circumference measuring 11ft (just over 3 metres).

There are so many ways you can decorate your cupcakes using buttercream, sugar paste and glacé icing. For more ideas see Chapter 14.

🧁 RED VELVET CUPCAKES 🧁

These cupcakes became incredibly popular in the USA and thanks to the trendy cupcakeries that seem to be springing up everywhere, they are fast becoming a favourite in the UK too. They have a distinctive red colour, hence the name, and are usually iced with cream cheese frosting.

Ingredients

(Makes 12)

- 125g plain flour
- $^1/_2$tsp salt
- 1tbsp cocoa powder
- 75g unsalted butter, softened
- 150g caster sugar
- $^1/_2$tsp vanilla extract
- A dash red food colour paste/1tbsp liquid red food colouring
- 1 egg
- 120ml buttermilk
- $^1/_2$tsp bicarbonate of soda
- 1tsp white wine vinegar

Method

1. Preheat the oven to 170°C (325°F or gas mark 3) and place 12 cupcake cases in a 12 hole muffin tin.

2. Sift the flour, salt and cocoa powder into a bowl and set to one side.

3. Cream together the butter, sugar and vanilla extract until light and fluffy, using a wooden spoon or food mixer.

4. Add the food colouring, the egg and 1tbsp of flour and mix together until it has all been incorporated.

5. Add half of the buttermilk along with half of the flour. Mix it all together. Repeat with the other half of the buttermilk and flour. Mix again until it has all been combined.

6. In a small bowl mix together the bicarbonate of soda and white wine vinegar. When the fizz begins to subside, add the mix to the cake batter, stir quickly to combine and spoon equal amounts into the cupcake cases.

Pocket tip 🍪

You need to work fairly swiftly to get the cupcakes in the oven as quickly as possible after adding the bicarbonate of soda — so make sure you have everything to hand before you add it to the mix.

7. Place the muffin tin in the centre of the oven and bake for 25–30 minutes until the cakes have risen and spring back when pressed gently in the centre.

8. Leave to cool in the tin for 5 minutes then remove them from the tin and allow to cool completely on a wire rack before decorating.

9. Decorate with cream cheese icing (p. 30) or vanilla butter-cream (p. 160).

🧁 MUFFINS 🧁

Muffins are the more rustic cousin of the cupcake. They usually rise higher with fuller tops and aren't usually decorated with fancy icing or frosting.

BANANA MUFFINS

Adding bananas to a cake recipe produces a wonderfully moist and dense texture. It is often a good idea to experiment with how much banana you add to your mixture so you can find the texture you like best. It's also a great recipe for using up those over ripe bananas from the fruit bowl that no-one fancies eating anymore!

Pocket fact -■-

Although we often refer to bananas growing on trees, they are actually the fruit of a herb plant.

Ingredients

(Makes 12)

- 115g unsalted butter
- 125g caster sugar
- 250g plain flour
- 2tsp baking powder
- 1tsp ground cinnamon
- 2 eggs
- 2 ripe bananas
- 200ml milk

Method

1. Preheat the oven to 180°C (350°F or gas mark 4) and grease a 12 hole muffin tin. You can use muffin cases if you'd prefer.

2. Melt the butter in a small saucepan over a low heat.

3. Measure the sugar into a bowl and sift in the flour, baking powder and cinnamon.

4. Once the butter has melted, transfer it to a large mixing bowl and whisk it together with the eggs and milk.

5. Add the dry ingredients and stir with a wooden spoon, making sure everything is combined.

6. Mash the bananas with a fork then stir them into the cake batter.

7. Divide the mixture equally between the 12 holes of the muffin tin and bake in the centre of the oven for around 20–25 minutes until a skewer inserted comes out clean.

8. Leave the muffins to cool in the tin for 5 minutes then gently run a knife around the edge of each one to loosen it. (If you are using muffin cases you won't need to do this.)

9. Leave to cool in the tin for another 5 minutes then remove to a wire rack to cool completely.

Variations to try

- *Add 2tbsp of sultanas for extra fruity banana muffins.*
- *Use a handful of chopped walnuts to add a nutty texture to your muffins.*

BLUEBERRY MUFFINS

These are delicious moist muffins, packed full of juicy fruit. It can be tricky to get the ratios right to begin with as too much fruit can leave the muffins a little soggy in the middle. With a little experimenting though you can easily produce the texture you like.

Pocket fact ◄■►

Blueberries are well known for their health benefits, containing a great deal of the anti-oxidants that are thought to combat cancer, heart disease and Alzheimer's.

Ingredients

(Makes 12)

- 200g plain flour
- 2tsp baking powder
- 150g caster sugar
- 150g blueberries
- 2 eggs
- 175ml milk
- 125ml vegetable oil

Pocket tip 🍪

If you are freezing fresh blueberries it's best to do so without washing them as this prevents the skins from becoming tough. Remember to give them a good rinse just before you are ready to use them.

Method

1. Preheat the oven to 170°C (325°F or gas mark 3) and grease the wells of a 12 hole muffin tin. You can use paper muffin cases if you prefer.

2. Sift the flour, saving back 1tbsp, and baking powder into a large bowl then stir in the sugar.

3. Wash the blueberries and put them into a separate bowl. Sprinkle the reserved tablespoon of flour over them and stir to make sure they are coated.

4. In a jug mix together the eggs, milk and vegetable oil.

Pocket tip 🍪

When making muffins it is best to keep the wet and dry ingredients separate until just before you are ready to mix the batter.

5. Pour the wet ingredients over the dry ingredients and stir to combine.

6. Add the blueberries and give the mixture a final stir to spread out the blueberries evenly.

7. Divide the cake batter equally between the 12 holes of the muffin tin and bake in the centre of the oven for 25–30 minutes until the muffins are well risen and golden in colour.

8. Leave the muffins to cool in the tins for 15 minutes but run a knife carefully around the edge of each muffin if you aren't using muffin cases.

9. Remove the muffins from the tin and leave to cool completely on a wire rack.

You can serve these muffins warm from the oven with custard or ice cream or leave them to cool to eat later. They will keep in an airtight container for a couple of days.

WHITE CHOCOLATE AND CRANBERRY MUFFINS

These tasty muffins have quite a Christmassy feel to them with the ruby red cranberries peeking through. Without the addition of the white chocolate and cranberries, this is also a useful basic muffin recipe that you can adapt to make lots of different types of muffin.

Pocket fact -■-

When cranberries are ripe they bounce because a small pocket of air forms. Because of this they are sometimes referred to as 'bounceberries'.

Ingredients

(Makes 9)

- 200g self-raising flour
- 1tsp baking powder
- 125g caster sugar
- 100ml sunflower oil
- 75ml milk
- 1 egg
- 75g white chocolate chips
- 75g dried cranberries

Method

1. Preheat the oven to 170°C (325°F or gas mark 3) and grease 9 holes of a 12 hole muffin tin. You can use paper muffin cases if you would prefer.

2. Sift the flour and baking powder into a large bowl.

3. Stir in the sugar.

4. In a jug mix the sunflower oil, milk and egg lightly with a fork just to break up the egg.

5. Add the oil mix to the dry ingredients and stir, making sure you don't over-beat the mixture.

6. Add the white chocolate chips and dried cranberries and give the cake batter one last stir.

7. Divide the mixture equally between the 9 holes or paper cases.

8. Bake in the centre of the preheated oven for 25–30 minutes until the muffins are well risen and a golden brown colour all over.

9. Remove them from the oven and run a knife carefully around the edge of each muffin to loosen it.

10. Cool in the tin for 15 minutes then remove the muffins to a wire rack to cool completely.

Store the muffins in cake tins or airtight containers and they will last for 2–3 days.

Variations to try

- *Replace the chocolate chips with milk or plain chocolate and try using different dried fruits, such as raisins or dried apricots.*
- *Make cherry and almond muffins by replacing the cranberries with chopped glacé cherries and the chocolate with chopped flaked almonds. Add $1/2$tsp almond extract to the mix too.*

🧁 WHOOPIE PIES 🧁

These cakey treats, sandwiched together with a delicious sweet filling, have started to become very popular and have been tipped to knock the cupcake from its top spot. A wide range of different flavoured whoopie pies are now available to buy in many cupcake shops and bakeries.

Pocket fact ‑■‑

Whoopie pies got their name from the Amish farmers who used to exclaim 'Whoopie!' with delight if they found one in their lunchbox.

Ingredients

(Makes 15)

- 300g plain flour
- 50g cocoa powder
- 1$\frac{1}{4}$tsp bicarbonate of soda
- 1tsp salt
- 250ml buttermilk
- 1tsp vanilla extract
- 115g unsalted butter, softened
- 215g soft light brown sugar
- 1 egg

For the filling

- 150g unsalted butter, softened
- 250g icing sugar
- $\frac{1}{4}$tsp vanilla extract

Method

1. Preheat the oven to 180°C (350°F or gas mark 4) and line 2 baking trays with greaseproof paper or baking parchment.

2. Sift together the flour, cocoa powder, salt and bicarbonate of soda in a large mixing bowl and leave to one side.

3. Mix together the buttermilk and vanilla extract in a small jug.

4. Cream together the butter and sugar in another bowl until well combined.

5. Add the egg and a tablespoon of flour to the butter mixture and mix with a wooden spoon until all the egg has been incorporated.

6. Alternately add the buttermilk and flour, a small amount at a time until it has all been added and mixed together to form a stiff cake batter.

Pocket tip 🍪

It can be useful to do the mixing in a food mixer if you have one as you can leave it running on a slow speed while you add the ingredients.

7. Place tablespoonfuls of the mixture onto the prepared baking trays, leaving enough room between each as they will spread slightly. If in doubt, test bake a few first to see how much they will spread.

8. Bake in batches for 15–18 minutes until they are risen and feel slightly springy when pressed gently.

9. Remove to cool completely on wire racks before making the filling to sandwich them together.

10. To make the filling, place the butter in a bowl, sift in the icing sugar and add the vanilla extract. Beat together to make a soft buttercream.

11. Spread or pipe the buttercream (see p.160) onto the flat side of one of the whoopie pie pieces then sandwich another one on top. Repeat to make 15 whoopie pies.

The whoopie pie halves will keep for several days unfilled in an airtight container and for 2 days when filled.

Variations to try

● *In the USA, the filling for whoopie pies often contains Marshmallow Fluff. This is starting to become more readily available in the UK from online stores such as www. americansweets.co.uk, www.ocado.com and from larger department stores. Try adding 4tbsp of Marshmallow Fluff to the filling recipe given above for a light fluffy filling.*

- Decorate the tops of the whoopie pies with some glacé icing and sprinkles, or sliced strawberries in the summer months.
- Make vanilla whoopie pies by replacing the cocoa powder with plain flour and add an extra $^1/_2$tsp vanilla extract.

Pocket fact ━■━

Whoopie pies are also sometimes referred to as 'gobs'. This term is thought to have stemmed from the small cakes miners would carry in their lunch buckets, which had the icing on the inside instead of the outside.

5

BREAD

The smell of fresh bread baking in the oven has to be one of the best ever. People often seem to have a fear of baking bread, thinking that it's labour intensive and difficult to get right, but actually it is very simple to mix up a batch of bread, all you need is time. Nowadays, bread machines are very popular and affordable and they can do all the work for you. In fact, you can even put the ingredients in, set the timer and have freshly baked bread ready for when you get up in the morning.

However, if you don't have a machine to do the work then you can easily make all these recipes by hand. All it takes is some mixing, kneading and time for the bread to rise.

Pocket tip 🍪

If you are using a bread machine to make your bread make sure you refer to the manufacturer's instructions so that you add the ingredients in the correct order. Some machines need liquids added first and others need the dry ingredients put in first.

All of the loaves described in this chapter will keep well for a couple of days if they are wrapped in foil or stored in an airtight container. Most can be enjoyed toasted when they start to lose their freshness.

Pocket tip 🍪

For a recipe for gluten-free bread see p.152.

🧁 SIMPLE WHITE LOAF 🧁

The basic white loaf is very easy to make, either by hand, with your food mixer or in a bread machine. Once you have perfected this you can begin to experiment with adding ingredients, making rolls or different shaped loaves.

Ingredients

(Makes a 2lb loaf)

- 500g strong white bread flour
- 2tsp salt
- 7g sachet fast-action dried yeast
- 2tsp caster sugar
- 3tbsp olive oil
- 300ml tepid water

Pocket tip 🍪

It's important to make sure your water isn't too hot or cold otherwise the yeast won't be effective. To get the correct temperature use one part boiling water to two parts cold water.

Method

1. Sift the flour into a large bowl, or the bowl of your food mixer if you are using this to make your dough. If you are using your bread machine then add the ingredients in the order recommended by the machine manufacturer.

2. Add the salt, sugar and yeast. Mix to combine and make a well in the centre.

3. Pour the oil into the well followed by the water.

4. Mix well with a wooden spoon to combine all the ingredients and make a dough. If you are using your food mixer it's best to use the dough hook attachment.

Pocket tip 🍪

It is often a good idea to add the water a small amount at a time as you may not always need the full quantity. You want the dough to be soft but not sticky.

5. Turn the dough out onto a lightly floured surface and knead for 8–10 minutes (5 minutes if you are using your food mixer to knead the dough) until it is smooth and elastic. The easiest way to do this is by pushing the dough away from you with the palm of one hand then rolling it back towards you. Turn the dough a quarter turn and repeat.

Pocket fact ▬■▬

Kneading the dough helps to make sure the yeast is evenly distributed, develops the gluten in the dough stopping it from becoming heavy and dense, and incorporates air, helping bubbles form in the dough, which expand and make the bread rise.

6. Place the dough in a large, lightly oiled bowl, cover with clingfilm and leave in a warm place to rise for an hour or until it has doubled in size.

7. Remove the dough from the bowl and gently knock it back by pressing down with your knuckles four or five times. This removes some of the air and redistributes the bubbles.

8. Shape the loaf by gently folding the edges under and place it in a lightly oiled 2lb loaf tin.

9. Cover with clingfilm and leave to rise again in a warm, draught-free place for 30–45 minutes until the dough has doubled in size again.

10. Preheat the oven to 200°C (400°F or gas mark 6) about 10–15 minutes before you are ready to bake the bread.

11. Once the dough is ready, bake the loaf for 25–30 minutes until it's risen and golden.

Pocket tip 🍪

A good way to test whether a loaf of bread is cooked is to tap the bottom gently. A hollow sound means it is ready. If there isn't a hollow sound return the loaf to the oven and test again after 5 minutes.

12. Leave in the tin to cool for 5 minutes then cool completely on a wire rack.

The loaf will keep fresh for a couple of days wrapped in foil or in an airtight container.

Pocket fact ▬■▬

The most popular bread in the UK is the white loaf, with 76% of the bread we buy and consume being white.

🧁 LIGHT WHOLEMEAL LOAF 🧁

The mixture of wholemeal and white bread flour in this loaf gives it a firmer texture. It's lovely served with slices of cheese or toasted and spread with butter and jam for breakfast.

Ingredients

(Makes a 2lb loaf)

- 350g wholemeal bread flour
- 150g strong white bread flour
- 1tsp salt
- 1tsp soft light brown sugar
- 7g sachet fast-action dried yeast
- 300ml tepid water

Method

1. Sift the flours and salt into a large bowl, tipping in any remaining bran from the sieve.

2. Stir in the sugar and yeast and make a well in the centre.

3. Add the water and mix to form a soft dough, either with a wooden spoon or with the dough hook attachment on a food mixer.

4. Turn the dough out onto a lightly floured surface and knead for 8–10 minutes (5 minutes if you use your food processor to do the kneading for you) until it is smooth and elastic.

5. Place the dough in a large, lightly oiled bowl, cover with clingfilm and leave to rise in a warm place for an hour or until it has doubled in size.

6. Lightly oil a 2lb loaf tin.

7. Gently knock the air out of the dough with your knuckles then form into a loaf shape and place into the tin.

8. Cover with oiled clingfilm and leave in a warm place again for 20–30 minutes until it is well risen.

9. Preheat the oven to 200°C (400°F or gas mark 6) 10–15 minutes before you plan to bake the loaf.

10. Dust the top of the loaf with a little wholemeal flour then bake in the centre of the oven for 25–30 minutes until the loaf is golden.

11. Leave to cool in the tin for 5 minutes before turning the bread out onto a wire rack to cool completely.

Pocket fact ▬
Sliced bread in the UK dates back to the mid-1930s and 80% of the bread we eat today is already sliced and wrapped.

🧁 SODA BREAD 🧁

This is a quick and simple loaf to make and is great served warm with some hearty soup or used for a tasty cheese ploughman's.

This is a yeast-free loaf, the raising agent being the bicarbonate of soda and buttermilk mix. Because of this you don't need to go through the lengthy double rising process like you do for many other loaves.

Ingredients

(Makes 1 medium loaf)

- 300g plain flour
- 200g plain wholemeal flour
- 1tsp bicarbonate of soda
- ½tsp salt
- 325ml buttermilk

Method

1. Preheat the oven to 200°C (400°F or gas mark 6) and line a baking tray with greaseproof paper or baking parchment.

Pocket tip

If you are using a good non-stick baking tray it will be sufficient to lightly dust it with some plain flour.

2. Sift the flours into a large bowl and tip in any bran remaining in the sieve.

3. Add the bicarbonate of soda and salt.

4. Gradually stir in the buttermilk to form a soft dough. You can either do this with a wooden spoon or use the dough hook attachment with your food mixer.

Pocket tip

If the dough seems too dry, add more buttermilk 1 tablespoon at a time.

5. Knead the dough for a couple of minutes until it becomes smooth, roll into a ball and place on the baking tray.

6. Gently press the ball of dough down to flatten slightly then with a sharp knife score the surface of the dough in one direction then the other to make a cross in the top.

7. Bake in the centre of a preheated oven for 30–35 minutes until the bread is risen and golden. Tap the bottom of the loaf to test if it sounds hollow.

8. Remove to a wire rack to cool completely.

Pocket fact ━■━

Looking at the total bread sales in the UK it averages out to 43 loaves per person purchased each year.

🧁 BRIOCHE 🧁

Brioche is a slightly sweet, French yeast bread, enriched with butter and eggs. It's often baked in small fluted tins with a top knot placed on top, but can easily be baked in muffin tins to save investing in more tins that may not get used often. Brioche is a delicious breakfast treat served warm with butter and jam and can also be baked with fillings such as dried fruit or chocolate chips.

Pocket fact ━■━

The origins of brioche are thought to date back as far as Roman times, although the first written reference to the word was in the early 1400s.

Ingredients

(Makes 12)

- 225g strong white bread flour
- Pinch salt
- 1tbsp caster sugar
- 7g sachet fast-action dried yeast

- 50g butter
- 2 eggs
- 1 beaten egg to glaze

Method

1. Sift the flour and salt into a large bowl or the bowl of your food mixer if you are using that to make the dough.

2. Add the sugar and yeast and stir to combine.

3. Melt the butter either in a small saucepan over a gentle heat or for 10 seconds at a time in the microwave.

4. Lightly beat the eggs and add them with the butter to the flour mix.

5. Stir with a wooden spoon or the dough hook attachment of your food mixer to make a soft, but not sticky, dough.

6. Turn out onto a lightly floured surface and knead for 5–7 minutes until it looks silky smooth and is elastic.

7. Place the dough into a large bowl that has been lightly oiled, cover with clingfilm and leave in a warm place for an hour until the dough has doubled in size.

Pocket tip 🍪

Some good warm places to consider for your rising dough are an airing cupboard, the laundry room when the tumble dryer has been running or turn your oven onto a low heat for 2 minutes then turn off and place the dough in there, leaving the door open.

8. Lightly grease a 12 hole muffin tin.

9. Gently knock the air out of the dough by pressing it down with your knuckles a few times, then divide it into 12 equal pieces.

10. Take three-quarters of the first piece of dough and form it into a round. Place it into one of the holes in the muffin tin.

Roll the smaller piece of dough into a round and place on top of the larger piece.

11. Push your finger down through the centre of the two rounds to make sure they stick together.

12. Repeat with the other 11 pieces of dough.

13. Cover the brioche with clingfilm and leave to rise again in a warm place for 30 minutes.

14. Preheat the oven to 200°C (400°F or gas mark 6) 10–15 minutes before you plan to bake the brioche.

15. Brush the tops of the brioche with the beaten egg and bake in the centre of the oven for 12–15 minutes until they are golden brown.

16. Leave to cool in the tins for 5 minutes before removing them to a wire rack to cool completely.

Pocket fact ◄■►

There are a vast number of different types of bread produced throughout the world, with at least 200 different types in the UK alone.

🧁 OLIVE BREAD 🧁

This delicious bread is packed full of olives and makes a lovely change from plain bread. It's especially tasty served warm and spread with butter. You can easily divide the dough and bake as rolls to add a bit of interest to children's lunchboxes or shape into various different loaves.

Ingredients

(Makes 1 medium loaf)

- 500g strong white bread flour
- 1tsp salt

- 1 tbsp caster sugar
- 7g sachet fast-action dried yeast
- 1 egg
- 200ml tepid water
- 50ml olive oil
- 12 black olives, cut into quarters

Method

1. Sift the flour and salt into a large bowl then stir in the sugar and yeast.

2. Make a well in the centre and add the egg, water and olive oil.

3. Add the olives, then stir with a wooden spoon or the dough hook attachment on the food mixer to make a dough.

4. Turn out the dough onto a lightly floured surface and knead for 8–10 minutes (or 5 minutes if you use the food mixer) until it is smooth and elastic.

5. Place in a lightly oiled bowl, cover with clingfilm and leave to rise in a warm place for an hour or until the dough has doubled in size.

6. Line a baking tray with greaseproof paper or baking parchment.

7. Knock the air out of the dough by pressing down with your knuckles a few times then shape the loaf into a long sausage shape, place on the baking tray and flatten slightly.

8. Cover with clingfilm and leave to rise in a warm place for a further 30–40 minutes.

9. Preheat the oven to 200°C (400°F or gas mark 6) about 10–15 minutes before you want to bake the loaf.

10. With a sharp knife score four lines in the top of the loaf at a 45° angle, dust with flour and bake in the centre of the oven for 25–30 minutes. Test the loaf is cooked by tapping the bottom to check if it sounds hollow.

11. Leave to cool on a wire rack.

🧁 SUNDRIED TOMATO AND 🧁 PARMESAN ROLLS

These rolls are delicious warm and spread with butter or cream cheese and are great in lunchboxes. You can also bake the dough as a loaf either in a 2lb loaf tin or shaped into a long or round loaf by hand.

Ingredients

(Makes 12)

- 25g sundried tomatoes
- 500g strong white bread flour
- 1tsp salt
- 1tsp caster sugar
- 7g sachet fast-action dried yeast
- 25g melted butter
- 300ml tepid water
- 40g finely grated parmesan

For the topping

- 25g melted butter
- 10g finely grated parmesan

Method

1. Soak the sundried tomatoes in warm water for 30 minutes then drain and roughly chop.

2. Sift the flour and salt into a large bowl then stir in the yeast and sugar.

3. Make a well in the centre and add the melted butter and water.

4. Add the parmesan and sundried tomatoes and stir to make a soft, but not sticky, dough.

5. Turn the dough out onto a lightly floured surface and knead for 8–10 minutes or 5 minutes if you are using a food mixer with dough hook attachment.

6. Place the dough in a lightly oiled bowl and leave to rise in a warm place for an hour or until it has doubled in size.

7. Line 2 baking sheets with greaseproof paper or baking parchment.

8. Knock out the air from the dough by pressing it a few times with your knuckles then divide it into 12 equal pieces and form each into a round roll shape.

9. Place the rolls on the baking sheets, leaving space between each for them to rise and expand.

10. Cover with oiled clingfilm and leave to rise for 20–30 minutes in a warm place.

11. Preheat the oven to 200°C (400°F or gas mark 6) 10–15 minutes before you want to bake the rolls.

12. Brush the tops of the rolls gently with melted butter and sprinkle with the parmesan.

13. Bake for 20–25 minutes until the rolls are golden.

14. Leave to cool on a wire rack.

6

BISCUITS AND COOKIES

Biscuits and cookies are hugely popular treats and snacks and it's easy to whip up a quick batch when you've got guests coming round. Once you've perfected a basic recipe you can experiment by adding different types of dried fruit, nuts, chocolate chips or fudge pieces. You can also try making smaller cookies from the recipes and sandwich them together with different fillings such as chocolate spread, buttercream or ganache.

> ### *Pocket fact* ━■━
>
> *The name for the flat, crunchy biscuits known as 'biscotti' literally means 'twice baked' in Italian and comes from the Latin* bis *meaning twice and* coctus *meaning cooked or baked.*

🧁 WHITE CHOCOLATE CHIP 🧁 COOKIES

This is a great, basic cookie dough that you can adapt to make lots of different flavoured cookies. If you want to ensure you have some dough ready to cook at short notice then make up double batches and freeze half of it. The easiest way to do this is to make the dough into balls and freeze them on a lined baking tray until they are hard then store them in freezer bags. You can then remove as many as you wish at a time and bake them straight from frozen, allowing a few minutes more baking time than you would for freshly made cookie dough.

Ingredients

(Makes 12—14)

- 150g unsalted butter
- 50g soft light brown sugar
- 75g caster sugar
- $^1/_2$tsp vanilla extract
- 1 egg
- 200g plain flour
- 150g white chocolate chips or chunks
- $^1/_2$tsp bicarbonate of soda

Pocket tip 🍪

Instead of using chocolate chips you can roughly chop white chocolate into chunks with a sharp knife.

Method

1. Preheat the oven to 180°C (350°F or gas mark 4) and line 2 baking sheets with greaseproof paper or baking parchment.

2. Place the butter, sugars and vanilla extract in a large bowl and cream together with a wooden spoon or in a food mixer.

3. Add the egg and beat to incorporate.

4. Sift together the flour and bicarbonate of soda into a separate bowl then gradually add it to the cookie mixture until it forms a dough.

5. Mix in the chocolate chips or chunks until they are well spread throughout the dough.

Pocket tip 🍪

Don't over-mix your cookie dough otherwise the cookies are likely to turn out too hard.

6. Divide the dough into 12–14 balls and space them well out on the prepared baking sheets. You don't need to flatten them as they will spread out as they bake.

7. Bake for 10–15 minutes until they are golden. They will still be soft when you take them out of the oven but will become firmer once they cool.

8. Leave them on the baking trays to cool for a couple of minutes then carefully remove the cookies to wire racks to cool completely.

Variations to try

- *Replace the white chocolate chips or chunks with plain or milk chocolate.*
- *Add 50g dried cranberries or chopped dried apricots to the dough mixture when you add the white chocolate for a fruity cookie.*
- *Replace 25g of the flour with cocoa powder to make tasty double chocolate chip cookies.*
- *For nutty choc chip cookies add 50g chopped hazelnuts or pecans to the dough when you add the chocolate chips.*

Pocket fact ▬■▬

There is an annual World Biscuit Throwing Championship in the UK where participants have to throw a rich tea biscuit as far as they can. Proceeds from the competition go to the NSPCC.

🧁 GINGER BISCUITS 🧁

These delicious crunchy ginger biscuits are sure to be a big hit with all the family. You can adjust the amount of ground ginger you use to suit your taste – children may not like it quite as spicy as adults!

Pocket fact ◦▬◦

Ginger is well known for its use in the kitchen and for its medicinal purposes. It's often used to help ease morning sickness, sea sickness and digestive discomfort.

Ingredients

(Makes 30)

- 100g unsalted butter
- 1tbsp golden syrup
- 100g soft light brown sugar
- 100g caster sugar
- 300g plain flour
- 2tsp baking powder
- 1tsp bicarbonate of soda
- 3tsp ground ginger
- 1 egg

Method

1. Preheat the oven to 160°C (200°F or gas mark 2) and line 2 large baking sheets with non-stick baking parchment or greaseproof paper.

2. Warm the butter, sugars and golden syrup in a saucepan over a gentle heat until the ingredients are combined. Set aside to cool for 5 minutes.

3. Sift together the flour, baking powder, bicarbonate of soda and ground ginger into a large bowl.

4. In a separate bowl, lightly whisk the egg with a fork.

5. Pour the butter and sugar mixture over the dry ingredients and add the egg. Mix together with a wooden spoon until it forms a soft dough. You can use a food mixer to do this if you have one.

6. Take walnut-sized pieces of the dough and roll into balls. Place the balls onto the prepared baking sheets and push them down with your fingers to make disc shapes.

Pocket tip 🍪

Don't place the discs too close together as they will spread a little as they bake. If you want to test how much your cookies will spread during baking, bake just a couple first. Then you'll know how best to space the remaining dough without any wasted space on the baking trays.

7. Bake for 15–20 minutes until the biscuits are a dark golden colour. They will still seem soft when you remove them from the oven but they will harden as they cool.

8. You may need to repeat steps 6 and 7 with another batch as the recipe makes 30 biscuits.

9. Leave the biscuits to cool on the trays for a couple of minutes then remove them to a wire rack to cool completely.

Pocket tip 🍪

Use a fish slice or large palette knife to carefully remove the biscuits from the tray.

These biscuits are perfect with a cup of tea or coffee in the afternoon. Store any left over biscuits in an airtight container and they will last for 3–4 days.

Pocket fact ▬

The 2008 Guinness Book of World Records *recognised a cookie baked by the Immaculate Baking Company in 2003 as the largest cookie in the world. It measured 100ft (about 30 metres) in diameter and weighed almost 40,000lb (about 18 tonnes).*

 CHOCOLATE CREAM BISCUITS

These are a firm family favourite and are also great to bake with children. They have a delicious chocolatey taste and are made using drinking chocolate instead of cocoa powder.

Pocket fact ◂■▶

Cocoa powder is made by crushing cocoa nibs, from the cocoa bean, to extract the cocoa butter. The remaining chocolate liquor is then dried and ground to make unsweetened cocoa powder.

Ingredients

(Makes 15)

- 225g baking margarine
- 115g caster sugar
- 1tsp vanilla extract
- 225g self-raising flour
- 55g drinking chocolate

Method

1. Preheat the oven to 180°C (350°F or gas mark 4) and line 2 baking sheets with greaseproof paper or baking parchment.

2. Cream together the baking margarine, sugar and vanilla extract in a bowl until well combined.

3. Sift together the flour and drinking chocolate in a separate bowl and add to the margarine and sugar mixture.

4. Mix together to form a soft dough with a wooden spoon or in a food mixer.

5. Divide the dough into pieces the size of walnuts, place onto the prepared baking sheets and flatten well with a fork – the more you flatten them, the crispier they will be.

Pocket tip 🍪

Dip the fork into a small pot of water before flattening each biscuit, then the biscuit dough won't stick to the fork.

6. Bake for 12–15 minutes.

7. Leave to cool on the trays for a couple of minutes then remove to wire racks to cool completely.

Variation to try

● *Make smaller biscuits and sandwich them together with some chocolate spread or chocolate buttercream.*

Pocket fact ━■━

The incredibly popular Oreo cookies, now available worldwide, were first produced by Nabisco in 1912 in New York City.

🧁 OAT AND SULTANA COOKIES 🧁

These soft oaty cookies are almost cakey in texture. You can experiment by adding your favourite types of dried fruit to them or even a few chocolate chips for a treat.

Pocket fact ━■━

Oats help to regulate the levels of glucose and insulin in the blood, which is especially useful for people with diabetes.

Ingredients

(Makes 15—18)

- 175g plain flour
- 1tsp mixed spice
- 150g rolled oats
- 125g soft light brown sugar
- 1 egg
- 150ml sunflower oil
- 50ml milk
- 2tbsp golden syrup
- 50g sultanas

Method

1. Preheat the oven to 180°C (350°F or gas mark 4) and line 2 baking sheets with greaseproof paper or baking parchment.

2. Sift the flour and mixed spice into a large bowl then add the oats and sugar. Mix with a wooden spoon to combine.

3. In a measuring jug lightly whisk together the egg, sunflower oil and milk with a fork or small whisk.

4. Add the golden syrup to the dry mixture then gradually add the egg and oil mixture, stirring to bring it all together.

5. Add the sultanas and give a final stir to incorporate them.

6. Place tablespoon-sized pieces onto the prepared trays, leaving space between them as they will spread during baking.

7. Bake for 15—20 minutes until they are golden brown. They will still be soft but will firm up as they cool.

8. Leave to cool for a couple of minutes on the tray then remove to a wire rack to cool fully.

The cookies will keep well in an airtight container for a couple of days. They are great as a lunchbox filler or an after-school snack as the oats slowly release energy, keeping children feeling full up for longer.

🧁 COCONUT MACAROONS 🧁

These sweet, chewy macaroons are a delicious treat with a mid-morning cup of coffee or afternoon tea. Macaroons can either be made using ground almonds or desiccated coconut and the pretty macaroons, made famous by Ladurée and Pierre Hermé, are fast becoming the trendy confectionery of choice.

These coconut macaroons are much easier to bake perfectly and are made using just three ingredients.

Ingredients

(Makes 20)

- 2 egg whites
- 100g caster sugar
- 160g desiccated coconut

Method

1. Preheat the oven to 160°C (320°F or gas mark 2) and grease and line 2 baking sheets with baking parchment or greaseproof paper.

Pocket tip 🍪

You can also line the baking sheets with rice paper, which will stick to the bottom of the macaroons and is edible.

2. Whisk the egg whites with an electric whisk until they become frothy. Be careful not to over-whisk them!

3. Add the sugar and desiccated coconut and stir with a wooden spoon or mix together with your hands.

4. Scoop lumps out of the mixture with a tablespoon, form into balls with your hands, place on the prepared baking sheets and flatten with your fingers to form discs, about 4cm across and 5mm in height.

5. Bake for 10–15 minutes until the macaroons have started to turn a golden brown colour.

6. Leave to cool for a few minutes on the sheets then carefully remove them to a wire rack to cool completely.

Pocket fact ━■━

Macaroons are often eaten by Jews during Passover because they are flourless and the leavening ingredient is egg whites, meaning they are suitable for the dietary restrictions in place during Passover.

🧁 PEANUT BUTTER COOKIES 🧁

You can use either smooth or crunchy peanut butter to bake these moreish cookies, but the crunchy version gives them a wonderful nutty texture. These cookies taste delicious when served with a glass of milk – you'll find that just one is never enough!

Ingredients

(Makes 18)

- 100g unsalted butter
- 100g peanut butter, crunchy or smooth
- 100g caster sugar
- 2tbsp golden syrup
- $^1/_2$tsp vanilla extract
- 200g plain flour
- $^1/_2$tsp bicarbonate of soda

Method

1. Preheat the oven to 180°C (350°F or gas mark 4). Line 2 baking sheets with greaseproof paper or baking parchment.

2. Cream together the butter, peanut butter and sugar in a bowl with a wooden spoon or in a food mixer.

3. Add the golden syrup and vanilla extract and mix together.

4. In a separate bowl, sift together the flour and bicarbonate of soda then gradually add it to the butter mixture until it forms a soft, but not sticky, dough.

5. Divide the dough into 18 balls, place them on the prepared trays and flatten with a fork, first in one direction then the other to make a criss-cross pattern.

Pocket tip 🧑

Don't place the balls of cookie dough too close together as they will spread out as they bake.

6. Bake in the preheated oven for 15–20 minutes until the cookies are a golden brown colour.

7. Leave to cool on the trays for a few minutes then remove to completely cool on wire racks.

Pocket tip 🍪

If cookies become soft, you can often crisp them up again by putting them in the oven on a low temperature for about 5 minutes.

Variations to try

- Chocolate and peanut butter always go well together. Add 50g milk chocolate chips or chopped chocolate to the cookie dough for delicious chocolate chip peanut butter cookies.
- Melt a 100g bar of dark chocolate and dip half of each cookie into it for a gorgeous chocolatey treat.

Pocket fact -■-

Peanuts aren't actually nuts, but legumes and are related to lentils and beans.

🧁 SHORTBREAD 🧁

Melt in the mouth shortbread is a very popular biscuit and is also incredibly versatile. It can be baked in a round and cut into triangles, baked in a rectangle and cut into fingers or cut into circles or squares with cookie cutters to make individual biscuits.

Pocket fact -■-

The name shortbread came about because of its crumbly texture, which is produced because of the high fat content in the recipe. 'Short' is an old fashioned word meaning 'crumbly'.

Ingredients

(Makes 12)

- 150g unsalted butter, softened
- 100g caster sugar (plus extra for dusting)
- Pinch of salt
- 250g plain flour

Method

1. Preheat the oven to 180°C (350°F or gas mark 4) and grease a shallow rectangular baking tin (preferably non-stick) measuring approximately 10 inches by 7 inches (25cm by 18cm).

2. Cream together the butter, sugar and salt in a mixing bowl until it's light and fluffy using either a wooden spoon or a food mixer.

3. Sift in the flour and combine it until it begins to form a soft dough.

4. It is usually best to use your hands to bring the dough together into one lump.

5. Press the dough into the prepared tin with your fingers and make sure it's spread out evenly.

6. Prick the surface all over with a fork and gently mark out the 12 fingers with a sharp knife.

7. Bake in the centre of the preheated oven for 25–30 minutes until the shortbread has started to turn a golden brown colour all over.

8. Remove from the oven and with a sharp knife cut through the marks you made before baking to divide the shortbread into 12 fingers.

9. Sprinkle with a little caster sugar and leave in the tin to cool completely before removing.

These shortbread fingers will go down brilliantly with a cup of tea in the afternoon. Try serving them on pretty plates with paper doilies to impress your friends when they are round for tea.

Variations to try

- For a delicious cherry shortbread mix 50g of glacé cherries into the dough before baking.
- Try adding a simple glacé icing to the shortbread before cutting it up. Just mix 100g of sifted icing sugar with a few teaspoons of water to make a thick icing to spread onto the shortbread. Once the icing has set, cut the shortbread into 12 fingers.
- Roll out the dough on a lightly floured work surface and cut out circles with a cookie cutter. Bake on a lined baking sheet and when they are cool, half dip them in melted dark or milk chocolate.

Pocket fact ▬

In 1991 McVitie's went to court to get Jaffa cakes classified as cakes and not biscuits so the company wouldn't have to pay VAT on them. McVitie's won the case.

7

TRADITIONAL BAKING

No matter how old you are, there are just some recipes that always remind you of home, and especially your mum. Many of them are good old traditional recipes, such as bread pudding and apple crumble, but all of them are comforting and bring back special memories. Now you can test out some of these recipes or find some of your own that your family will treasure for generations to come.

🧁 BREAD PUDDING 🧁

Pocket fact -■-

Bread pudding dates back to the 13th century when it was known as 'poor man's pudding'. It was invented to use up left-over stale bread and was mixed with some water, sugar and spices, meaning it was cheap to make. Gradually more ingredients were added to make the pudding we know today.

Ingredients

(Serves 8)

- 225g bread (preferably a few days old or stale)
- 45g glacé cherries
- 45g currants
- 75g sultanas
- 1tsp mixed spice
- 50g caster sugar (plus extra for dusting)
- 1 egg

- 45ml milk
- Butter for greasing flan dish

Method

1. Break the bread into chunks, place it in a large bowl and cover with water. Leave it to soak for an hour.

2. Preheat the oven to 180°C (350°F or gas mark 4) and butter the bottom and sides of an 8 inch (about 20 cm) flan dish.

3. Squeeze out the water from the bread and place the bread in another bowl.

4. Cut the glacé cherries into quarters and add them to the bread. Wash the currants and sultanas and also add to the bread. Mix with a fork to combine the bread and the fruit.

5. Add the sugar and mixed spice and mix again.

6. In a measuring jug whisk together the milk and the egg, then add it to the bread mixture.

7. Stir the mix again and pour into the prepared flan dish. Level the surface with the fork.

8. Bake in the centre of the oven for 20–25 minutes until the top is golden and the pudding is just firm.

9. Remove from the oven and sprinkle with a little extra caster sugar.

Lovely served warm or cold the next day. Refrigerate any left-overs.

🧁 SCONES 🧁

Scones are the perfect summer treat and are wonderful served as part of afternoon tea, thickly spread with strawberry jam and clotted cream. They hold strong memories of lazy summer holidays, with picnics in the fields and long days playing out in the sunshine.

Pocket fact -■-

Some pronounce it 'skon', rhyming with 'John' but some say 'skohn', rhyming with 'cone' — who is correct?

Ingredients

(Makes 8)

- 250g self-raising flour
- Pinch of salt
- 50g caster sugar
- 50g unsalted butter, chilled
- 1 large egg
- 100ml milk

Method

1. Preheat the oven to 200°C (400°F or gas mark 6) and line a baking tray with greaseproof paper or baking parchment.

2. Sift the flour into a large bowl and stir in the sugar and salt.

3. Dice the butter and add to the flour. Rub the butter into the flour either using your fingers or a pastry blender until it resembles fine breadcrumbs. Alternatively, you can do this using a food processor.

4. Beat the egg and milk together in a jug, then add it gradually to the flour mixture to form a dough. If the mixture is still crumbly then add more milk, a little at a time.

Pocket tip 🧍

You may not need all the milk and egg so add it slowly. If you add too much you will end up with a sticky dough that is diffi-cult to handle.

5. Bring the dough together using your hands and form it into a ball. Turn it out onto a lightly floured surface and pat down to a thickness of approximately 3cm.

6. Using a 6cm round cookie cutter, cut out 8 scones and place them on the baking sheet, leaving enough space between each for them to rise and expand a little.

Pocket tip 🎅

When cutting out the scones make sure you push the cutter straight down and don't twist it, otherwise it seals the edges and the scones won't rise evenly.

7. Brush the tops of the scones with any leftover egg and milk mixture and bake in the centre of the oven for 10–12 minutes until they are risen and golden on top.

Pocket tip 🎅

Be careful not to let any of the egg and milk run down the sides of the scone as this will also stop them from rising evenly.

8. Remove the scones from the baking tray and cool completely on a wire rack.

Scones are especially delicious served with jam and clotted cream. They are best eaten on the day they are baked as they dry out quickly, but they freeze well so you can bake a batch ahead of time and defrost them when you need them.

Variations to try

- *For fruity scones add 50g washed sultanas and 1tsp cinnamon to the dough.*
- *To make some naughty, but nice, chocolate chip scones add 50g plain chocolate chips or chopped chocolate to your scone dough.*
- *For a Christmassy twist add 50g white chocolate chips and 50g dried cranberries to the scone mix.*

🧁 HOT CROSS BUNS 🧁

These fruity, spiced buns are marked with a pastry cross on the top and traditionally served on Good Friday. The cross is meant to symbolise the crucifixion of Jesus, although there are some who think they date back further than this. Hot cross buns are delicious served warm or toasted and spread with butter and can be a warming treat at any time of the year.

Ingredients

(Makes 12)

- 450g strong white bread flour
- 2tsp ground mixed spice
- 1tsp ground cinnamon
- 1/2 tsp salt
- 50g caster sugar
- 7g sachet fast-action dried yeast
- 50g butter, melted
- 1 egg
- 200ml warm milk
- 50g raisins
- 50g sultanas
- 25g mixed peel

For the pastry crosses
- 50g plain flour
- 25g butter, melted
- Water

For the glaze
- 2tbsp milk
- 25g caster sugar

Method

1. Sift the flour, spices, cinnamon and salt into a large bowl then stir in the yeast and sugar.

2. Lightly beat the egg then add it along with the melted butter to the flour mix.

3. Begin to stir the ingredients together with your fingers or a palette knife, gradually adding the warm milk as you go, until the dough comes together into a ball. You may not need all the milk or you may need a little more.

4. Turn the dough out onto a lightly floured surface and knead for 10 minutes until the dough has become silky and elastic.

5. Place the dough in a large, lightly oiled bowl, cover with clingfilm and leave in a warm place to rise for an hour.

6. Line a large baking tray with greaseproof paper or baking parchment.

7. Turn out the dough onto a floured surface and knock the air out of it. Knead in the dried fruit and mixed peel until they are evenly distributed throughout the dough. This can be hard work, but keep going!

8. Divide the dough into 12 equal pieces and put them on the prepared baking tray, leaving room for them to rise and swell. Cover with clingfilm and put in a warm place again for 30 minutes or until they have doubled in size.

9. Preheat the oven to 200°C (400°F or gas mark 6) 15 minutes before you want to bake the hot cross buns.

10. To make the pastry for the crosses, rub the butter into the flour then mix in enough water to make the pastry into a pipeable consistency.

11. Spoon the pastry into a piping bag, snip the end and pipe a cross on the top of each bun.

12. Bake in the centre of the oven for 15–20 minutes until the buns are golden brown.

13. To make the glaze, place the milk and sugar in a small saucepan and heat until the sugar has dissolved. Brush the glaze over the warm buns with a pastry brush and leave to cool on a wire rack.

🧁 APPLE CRUMBLE 🧁

What could be more comforting than mum's apple crumble? This feel good food is so easy to whip up and is the perfect end to a Sunday lunch, served warm with ice cream or custard. It is also a great way to use up the glut of autumn apples if you have your own trees.

Pocket tip 🧍

Prepare and stew the apples then freeze them in smaller batches. Just get out what you need for your pies and crumbles the night before.

Ingredients

(Serves 6)

- 750g cooking apples (weight before preparing), such as Bramley
- Lemon juice
- 50g caster sugar

For the crumble

- 300g plain flour
- 200g unsalted butter
- 2tsp cinnamon
- 100g demerara sugar

Method

1. Preheat the oven to 180°C (350°F or gas mark 4) and grease a 9 inch (24cm) ovenproof dish.

2. Peel and core the apples and cut them into large chunks.

3. Place them in a medium-sized saucepan and sprinkle with lemon juice to stop them going brown and then add 1tbsp water. Turn the hob onto a low heat and stew the apples for about 5 minutes until they are tender but haven't broken down.

4. Stir in the sugar to taste.

5. In the meantime, make the crumble topping in a large bowl by rubbing the butter into the flour until it resembles coarse breadcrumbs.

6. Stir in the sugar and cinnamon.

7. Place the apples in the ovenproof dish and sprinkle with the crumble topping. Bake in the centre of the oven for 20–25 minutes until the top has turned golden.

8. Leave to cool for 5 minutes before serving.

Store leftovers covered in the fridge. If you fancy making up a double batch of crumble topping, you can freeze half of it ready for next time you want to make a crumble.

🧁 PINEAPPLE UPSIDE-DOWN 🧁 PUDDING

This is a warm, comforting pudding with a special twist when you turn it out of the bowl. The tangy pineapple and sweet cherries will make a colourful top to the pudding as well as tasting delicious. Be sure to turn it out at the table to impress your family or dinner guests and serve with lashings of fresh custard.

Ingredients

(Serves 6)

- 2tbsp golden syrup
- 4 pineapple rings
- 5 glacé cherries
- 200g butter or baking margarine, softened

- 200g caster sugar
- 2tbsp milk
- 1tsp vanilla extract
- 3 eggs
- 200g self-raising flour
- 1tsp baking powder

Method

1. Preheat the oven to 170°C (325°F or gas mark 3) and grease a 7 inch (18cm) square ovenproof dish and spread the golden syrup in the bottom.

2. Place the pineapple rings in the bottom of the bowl with a cherry in each of the rings and another in the middle where the rings touch.

3. Cream together the butter or baking margarine and sugar in a mixing bowl with a wooden spoon until it's pale and well mixed.

4. Beat the eggs, milk and vanilla extract together in a jug.

5. Sift together the flour and baking powder in a separate bowl.

6. Add half the egg mixture and half the flour to the butter and sugar and mix together well. Repeat with the rest of the eggs and flour and mix until it is well combined.

Pocket tip 🍪

If you are using a food processor you can add all the ingredients at once and mix for 2 minutes using a beater attachment.

7. Spoon the cake batter over the pineapple and cherries in an ovenproof dish and bake in the centre of the oven for 30–35 minutes, until the sponge is well risen and golden, and a skewer inserted into the centre comes out clean.

8. Leave to cool for 5 minutes, then loosen the sponge round the edge with a palette knife.

9. Place a plate over the top of the dish and invert so the sponge is sitting the other way up on the serving plate and the pineapple is on the top.

Pocket tip 🎄

Make sure you use oven gloves and turn the pudding over carefully — it will be very hot!

Any leftovers will keep in the fridge until the next day and are delicious reheated or served cold.

Pocket fact ▬

Pineapples first made an appearance in the UK in 1660.

8

COMFORT BAKING

When it's cold outside or you've had a bad day, baking something delicious can really lift your mood. In this section are some recipes that are guaranteed to put a smile on your face. From warming suet pudding to sweet chewy flapjack there is something here that is sure to please the whole family.

The act of baking can also be therapeutic and these recipes are simple but with just enough challenge to get you busying around the kitchen, forgetting your troubles.

🧁 CHOCOLATE FUDGE CAKE 🧁

This rich, moist chocolate cake is sure to put a smile on anyone's face. The gooey cake is delicious served warm with cream or ice cream or cold with a cup of tea for an afternoon treat.

Ingredients

(Serves 8—10)

- 175g unsalted butter, softened
- 175g soft dark brown sugar
- 1tbsp golden syrup
- 150g self-raising flour
- 1tsp baking powder
- 25g cocoa powder
- 3 eggs

For the fudge icing and filling

- 100g butter
- 4tbsp milk

- 2tbsp cocoa powder
- 250g icing sugar, sifted

Method

1. Preheat the oven to 170°C (325°F or gas mark 3). Grease and line a 7 inch (18cm) round deep cake tin.

Pocket tip 🍪

You could bake the cake in 2 sandwich tins instead to save you splitting it later. You will need to reduce the cooking time to 25–30 minutes.

2. Cream together in a mixing bowl the butter and sugar with a wooden spoon or in a food mixer, then stir in the golden syrup.

3. Beat the eggs in a jug with a fork or small whisk.

4. Sift together the flour, cocoa powder and baking powder into a separate bowl.

5. Add half the eggs and half the flour mix to the butter and sugar and mix well.

6. Repeat with the rest of the eggs and flour and mix until the ingredients are well combined.

7. Spoon the cake batter into the prepared tin and bake in the centre of the oven for 45–55 minutes until a skewer inserted into the centre comes out clean.

8. Leave the cake to cool in the tin for half an hour and then remove from the tin and place on a wire rack to cool completely.

9. To make the icing, place the butter, milk and sifted cocoa powder into a medium-sized saucepan and heat gently until the butter has melted.

Pocket tip 🍪

If the icing mixture looks like it has split or is in danger of splitting then whisk it for a minute with a small whisk until it comes back together.

10. Remove the pan from the heat and allow to cool for 5 minutes before sifting in the icing sugar a quarter at a time. Beat vigorously after each addition of icing sugar until it's all combined. If you want the icing a bit stiffer, add more icing sugar 1tbsp at a time.

11. Leave to cool until you are ready to use it, beating occasionally.

12. Split the cake in half with a serrated knife and fill with one-third of the icing. Spread the remaining icing on the top and around the sides of the cake.

This cake will last for a few days (if you're lucky!) and is best stored in the fridge.

Pocket fact ▪️▪️

The melting point of chocolate is just below human body temperature, meaning chocolate melts in the mouth and releases endorphins in the brain, chemicals which produce the feel good factor.

Variations to try

• *If you are in a hurry and don't have time to make the chocolate fudge icing, whip up a batch of chocolate buttercream instead (see p.160 for the buttercream recipe).*

• *You can turn this into a divine birthday cake by decorating it with chocolate treats such as flakes, Smarties, chocolate buttons and white chocolate shavings.*

🧁 JAM ROLY POLY 🧁

This is a real old-fashioned pudding, often fondly associated with memories of school dinners. The suet crust is easy to make up as a speedy pudding and you can fill it with any jam of your choice. Nowadays you can get vegetable suet, which is lower in fat and is suitable for vegetarians.

Pocket fact ▬

Jam roly poly is also sometimes known as 'dead man's leg' (due to its pale appearance after steaming) and dates back to the early 19th century. It was also often referred to as 'shirt sleeve pudding' in the past as it was rolled up and steamed in an old shirt sleeve!

Ingredients

(Serves 6–8)

- 250g self-raising flour
- 125g shredded vegetable suet
- Pinch of salt
- 5–6tbsp water
- 3tbsp raspberry jam
- 1tbsp milk
- 1 egg
- Caster sugar to sprinkle

Method

1. Preheat the oven to 180°C (350°F or gas mark 4) and line a baking tray with greaseproof paper or baking parchment.

2. Sift the flour into a large bowl and add the salt and suet.

3. Add enough water to make a soft, but not sticky, dough using a wooden spoon or your hands.

4. Lightly flour the work surface and roll out the dough with a non-stick rolling pin to make a rectangle approximately 8 inches by 12 inches (20cm by 30cm).

5. Place the jam in a small microwaveable bowl and warm on a medium heat in the microwave for 20 seconds.

6. Spread the jam over the suet pastry leaving a 2cm border around all the edges.

7. Brush milk along the border and fold the edges over just to neaten them up.

8. Roll the pastry up from one of the short edges, not too tightly, and place on the baking tray with the seam underneath.

9. Beat the egg in a small bowl with a fork and use a pastry brush to moisten the top of the roly poly. Sprinkle all over with caster sugar.

10. Bake in the centre of the oven for 35–40 minutes until the pudding is golden.

11. Remove from the oven and leave to cool for 5 minutes before serving warm with custard.

You can keep any leftovers in the fridge and warm them up in the oven the next day.

Pocket fact ◄■►

One of the first written mentions of suet in a recipe was in 1617. It was listed as an ingredient in 'Cambridge Pudding', which was served to the students in the Cambridge halls of residence.

🧁 APPLE PIE 🧁

A good old apple pie is always sure to be a crowd pleaser and is the perfect end to a Sunday roast dinner. You can stew plenty of apples when they are in abundance and freeze in batches, defrosting what you need on the day you want to use it.

Pocket fact ◄■►

Apples have been around for more than 4,000 years and have been grown in the UK since Roman times.

Ingredients

(Serves 6–8)

For the filling
- 3–4 large Bramley apples (approximately 1kg)
- 2–3tbsp caster sugar to taste
- 1tsp cinnamon
- Lemon juice

For the pastry
- 300g plain flour
- 100g vegetable fat
- 50g baking margarine or butter
- 4–5tbsp cold water

Method

1. Begin by making the filling for the apple pie. Peel and core the apples. Cut them into quarters then each quarter in half and half again.

2. Place the apples in a saucepan and sprinkle with lemon juice as you go.

Pocket tip 🧍

Sprinkling cut apples with lemon juice will help to stop them from going brown before you cook them.

3. Cook the apples over a gentle heat for 10–15 minutes until they are soft but haven't lost their shape.

4. Turn off the heat and stir in enough sugar to taste and 1tsp cinnamon.

5. Set the filling to one side to cool while you make the pastry.

6. Sift the flour into a large bowl, add the vegetable fat and baking margarine and rub it in using your finger tips or a pastry blender. You can also do this in a food processor.

Pocket tip 🧍

If you are using a food processor to make your pastry make sure you don't over-work it as this can make the pastry tough.

7. Once the fat and flour mixture resembles fine breadcrumbs, mix in the cold water, a tablespoon at a time. You may need more or less water than the recipe states so make sure you add it gradually.

8. Mix in the water using your fingers until it begins to come together to form a ball.

9. Wrap the pastry in clingfilm and chill in the fridge for 30 minutes to 1 hour.

10. Preheat the oven to 180°C (350°F or gas mark 4) 15 minutes before you plan to bake the apple pie. Make sure to grease the pie dish first so that the pie comes out easily at the end.

11. Once the pastry has chilled turn it out onto a lightly floured surface and roll out two-thirds of it into a large circle and place it in a pie dish. Gently use the side of your finger to smooth the pastry into the pie dish and trim the excess from the edges.

Pocket tip 🧍

If you are struggling to roll out your pastry because it is a little crumbly, try rolling it on a piece of greaseproof paper so that you can lift it off the work surface more easily.

12. Fill the pie dish with the cooled apple filling.

13. Roll out the rest of the pastry to make the lid. Moisten around the edge of the pastry case with a little water and drape the pastry over the top.

14. Press the edges firmly together and trim off the excess pastry. You can crimp the edges by pressing down with a fork or by using two fingers of one hand and one on the other to push the edges together.

15. Use a sharp knife to make two slits in the centre of the pie lid.

Pocket tip 🧍

If you have any leftover pastry, make some shapes using cookie cutters to go on the top. This is a great job for children to join in with. Use a dab of water to stick the shapes onto the pastry lid.

16. Brush with a little milk and sprinkle with caster sugar.

17. Bake in the centre of the oven for 30–35 minutes until the pastry is golden.

Apple pie is best served warm with custard, ice cream or cream, but delicious cold the next day too. Store any leftovers in the fridge and eat within 2 days.

Pocket fact ‑■‑

There are over 7,500 different varieties of apple worldwide.

🧁 FLAPJACK 🧁

Made from just a few store cupboard ingredients, flapjack is an easy and moreish snack to bake in a hurry. It's also a great recipe to bake with the children and they can take slices of it with them in their lunchboxes the next day. The soft brown sugar in this recipe produces a deliciously chewy flapjack with a syrupy flavour.

Pocket fact ‑■‑

The word flapjack dates back to the early 17th century but was used to describe a dish more like a pancake or flat tart. It wasn't until 1935 that the word was used to describe the oaty snack we enjoy today.

Ingredients

(Makes 12 pieces)

- 75g unsalted butter
- 2tbsp golden syrup
- 125g soft light brown sugar
- 175g rolled oats

Method

1. Preheat the oven to 180°C (350°F or gas mark 4) and grease a small baking tray, approximately 8 inches by 9 inches (18cm by 23cm).

2. Place the butter, sugar and syrup in a fairly large saucepan and heat gently until the butter has melted and the ingredients are well combined.

3. Stir in the oats until they are completely coated by the syrupy mixture.

4. Press the mixture into the prepared tin using the back of a metal spoon and bake in the centre of the oven for 20 minutes until the flapjack is golden.

5. Allow the flapjack to cool for 10 minutes then mark out the squares with a sharp knife. This will make it easier to cut the flapjack when it is cool.

6. Leave to cool completely then remove from the tray.

Stored in an airtight container, the flapjack will last well for several days.

Variations to try

- Add 50g of washed raisins, sultanas or chopped apricots to the mixture with the oats for a fruity flapjack.
- Mix in 50g chocolate chips or chopped chocolate before baking the flapjack. Milk chocolate works particularly well.
- When the flapjack has cooled, melt some chocolate in a bowl over a saucepan of gently simmering water and drizzle over the flapjack, or spread a thin layer all over the top.

🧁 SWISS ROLL 🧁

Swiss roll, also known as jelly roll in the USA, is a thin rectangle of whisked sponge cake spread with filling, rolled up and cut into slices to serve. You can jazz up a simple Swiss roll with a variety of different fillings and change it from a simple teatime treat into an impressive after-dinner roulade.

Pocket fact ▬

Despite its name, the Swiss roll didn't actually originate in Switzerland. It's more likely to have come from Germany or Austria.

Ingredients

(Serves 8)

- 3 eggs
- 75g caster sugar (plus extra for sprinkling)
- $^1/_2$tsp vanilla extract
- 75g plain flour
- $^1/_2$tsp baking powder
- Icing sugar for dusting

Method

1. Preheat the oven to 180°C (350°F or gas mark 4) and line a shallow 8 inch by 13 inch (20cm by 32cm) Swiss roll tin with greaseproof paper or baking parchment.

2. Whisk the eggs and sugar in a mixing bowl with an electric whisk for 7–8 minutes until they have become pale and greatly increased in volume.

3. Add the vanilla extract. Sift in the flour and baking powder and fold into the mixture using a metal spoon. Be careful not to over-mix the cake batter or you will knock all the air out of it.

4. Pour the mixture into the prepared tin and gently tilt the tin to make sure the batter is evenly spread out.

5. Bake for 10–15 minutes until the cake is golden and set.

6. Place a piece of greaseproof paper on the work surface and sprinkle with caster sugar. Turn the Swiss roll onto the paper and peel off the lining paper from the cake.

7. Starting at one of the long edges, roll up the Swiss roll, with the paper in it, and leave to cool completely.

Pocket tip 🍪

Rolling up the sponge while it is still warm will help it take on the rolled shape and prevent it from cracking later.

8. Once it's cool, unroll the cake and remove the paper. Spread with your choice of filling and roll back up. Dust with icing sugar and cut into pieces to serve.

Swiss roll in five other languages

- *Danish – Roulade*
- *Norwegian – Rullekake*
- *Swedish – Rulltårta*
- *Spanish – Pionono*
- *French – Gâteau roulé*

Variations to try

- *Spread the unrolled Swiss roll with buttercream then top with lemon curd. Roll up and serve dusted with icing sugar.*
- *Replace 15g of the flour with cocoa powder and fill with dark or white chocolate buttercream.*
- *Fill with whipped cream and chopped fresh fruit, such as strawberries, raspberries or mandarin orange segments to make a tasty roulade dessert.*

🧁 SYRUP SPONGE PUDDING 🧁

Traditional steamed puddings take time to cook and fill the house with a delicious aroma as they do so, but nowadays it's easy to cheat and knock up a sponge pudding like this in the microwave in minutes. While it may not seem like traditional baking, we all lead busy lives and it is always good to have a pudding that you know you can have on the table with little effort and in a very short time. Sometimes cheating is good!

Pocket fact -■-

The word pudding is used not only to describe sweet desserts but also savoury dishes, such as steak and kidney pudding and Yorkshire pudding.

Ingredients

(Serves 4–6)

- 2tbsp golden syrup
- 115g baking margarine
- 115g caster sugar
- 115g self-raising flour
- $^1/_2$tsp vanilla extract
- 2 eggs

Method

1. Grease a 2 pint (1.2 litre) Pyrex or microwaveable pudding bowl. Drizzle the golden syrup around the sides and bottom of the bowl.

2. Cream together in a mixing bowl the baking margarine and sugar with a wooden spoon until light and fluffy.

Pocket tip 🍪

If you have a food mixer you can use the all-in-one method to make this pudding. Simply place all of the ingredients into the bowl of your food mixer and beat with the beater blade for a minute until it is all combined.

3. Add the vanilla extract, one of the eggs and sift in half the flour. Beat again with the wooden spoon.

4. Repeat with the other egg and the rest of the flour and beat until the ingredients are well combined.

5. Pour the mixture into the pudding bowl, cover with a microwave-safe plate and cook in the microwave on high power for $3^{1}/_{2}$ to 4 minutes.

6. Leave to cool for 1 minute, loosen around the edge with a knife then turn out onto a plate. Serve warm with custard.

Pocket tip 🍪

If you want to steam the pudding, cover the pudding bowl with greaseproof paper and then foil, and tie with some string. Steam in a large saucepan for 2 hours, making sure the water level is always half way up the pudding bowl.

Variations to try

- *For a lovely jam pudding, replace the syrup with 2–3 table-spoons of your favourite jam.*
- *Make a chocolatey pudding by replacing 15g of the flour with cocoa powder. Serve with chocolate custard.*
- *Try adding some steamed fruit, such as apples or summer berries, to the bottom of the pudding bowl instead of the syrup.*

9

PASTRIES

There are several different types of pastry, with the four main types listed below – some are a little more difficult to make than others. With the ready-made selection available in the supermarkets today the temptation is just to buy a pack, and for some pastries, such as filo, this is probably a good idea! However, a simple pastry, such as shortcrust, is actually very easy to make and will be a lot cheaper to make than to buy.

Some pastries, such as puff pastry, are fairly time consuming to make, but if you plan this into your schedule then they aren't so difficult after all. Just think of the sense of achievement when you have produced a pastry dish from scratch without cheating and buying it ready-made from the supermarket.

Having said that, our lives are busy nowadays and there is nothing wrong with a little cheating now and then. You can always spend your time perfecting the perfect filling for your pie and buy a pack of pastry for speed once in a while.

🧁 SHORTCRUST PASTRY 🧁

Shortcrust pastry is probably the easiest type of pastry to make and can be used for sweet and savoury dishes. Sometimes you can add a little sugar to the mix for sweet tarts and occasionally the pastry is enriched with an egg. The most basic type of shortcrust pastry is made from plain flour, salt, butter (or a mixture of vegetable fat and butter) and water to bind the mixture together.

Shortcrust pastry is usually used for making pie crusts and tart cases, such as in the cherry pie and Bakewell tart recipes in this chapter.

🧁 PUFF PASTRY 🧁

Puff pastry is also a very popular pastry, especially for making pie lids and sweet tarts, but is more time consuming to make. It's also trickier to master than shortcrust pastry, but by no means impossible. Make sure you leave yourself plenty of time for the first few attempts, but it will be well worth the wait.

This pastry is made by rolling a pastry mix and butter together, while folding the pastry in a certain way between each roll. It also needs to be chilled between each set of folds and must only be rolled in one direction at a time.

Puff pastry is also great for making sweet pastries, such as apple turnovers, vol au vent cases and pastry tarts such as the plum and almond tart in this chapter.

🧁 CHOUX PASTRY 🧁

This is another type of pastry that is quite simple to make. It involves heating butter and water together before quickly beating in the flour to make a thick paste. Finally beaten eggs are added, a little at a time, until you get the correct consistency.

It can be spooned onto baking sheets to make profiteroles, as in the profiterole recipe, or piped into longer shapes to make chocolate éclairs. If you are feeling particularly artistic, you can also pipe it to make swan shapes (see p. 129 for piping techniques). The hollow centre is usually filled with flavoured whipped cream or crème pâtissière (also known as pastry cream) and the tops covered in sauce. So it's brilliantly easy to make but is sure to impress your friends when they come round for dinner or afternoon tea.

🧁 FILO PASTRY 🧁

Filo pastry, also known as phyllo, is the tricky one of the bunch, but you can master it with a lot of patience and practice. Filo is used in wafer-thin sheets, spread with butter between each layer, to make sweet or savoury tarts, and is especially popular in Greek, eastern European and Middle Eastern cooking.

Filo pastry is made from flour, water and oil, and needs a lot of rolling and stretching to make it paper thin and needs resting between the rolling. This is a great pastry for the more experienced baker who is looking for a challenge.

🧁 CHERRY PIE 🧁

You can use the basic sweet shortcrust pastry in this recipe as the starting point for any fruit pie or tart recipe. Use your favourite fruit, or whichever fruits are in season, to experiment with and add different spices to suit your taste.

Ingredients

(Serves 8)

- 350g plain flour
- Pinch of salt
- 25g caster sugar
- 200g unsalted butter
- 1 egg
- 1tbsp water

For the filling

- 500g cherries, stoned
- 1tsp cinnamon
- 1tbsp cornflour
- 2tbsp caster sugar

Method

1. Sift the flour and salt into a large bowl then dice the butter and add it.

2. Rub the butter into the flour using your fingertips or a pastry blender until it resembles fine breadcrumbs. You can also use a food processor to do this.

3. Stir in the sugar.

4. Beat together the egg and water in a jug then add it, a little at a time, to the flour mix. Use your hands or a palette knife to

stir the dough and bring it together into a ball. If the pastry is dry, add a little more water.

5. Wrap the ball of pastry in some clingfilm and chill for 30 minutes in the fridge.

Pocket tip 👤

It's important to chill the pastry before using it as this gives it time to relax and for the liquid to be absorbed, meaning your pastry will be easier to handle and less likely to shrink when you bake it.

6. Preheat the oven to 180°C (350°F or gas mark 4).

7. Dust the work surface with a little flour then roll out half the pastry until it is about 3mm thick. Line a pie dish or plate with it and trim off any excess pastry.

8. Toss the cherries in the cornflour and cinnamon and spoon over the pastry. Sprinkle the sugar over the top.

9. Roll out the remaining pastry to make the pie lid. Moisten around the edge of the pastry base with a wet finger then lay the lid on top, press down around the edges to seal and trim off any excess pastry.

10. Crimp the edge with a fork and make two slits in the lid with a sharp knife.

11. Brush the top of the pie with some beaten egg or milk and bake in the centre of the oven for 30–35 minutes until the pastry is golden and the cherries are soft.

12. Serve warm with custard or ice cream.

Variations to try

- *For an extra special treat, try soaking the cherries in a table-spoon of Kirsch for a couple of hours before using them in the pie filling.*

> - *Peel and chop up 3—4 large Bramley apples and stew them over a gentle heat until they are soft. Add sugar to taste and use as the filling for your pie. You could also add 1tsp of cinnamon and a handful of washed sultanas too.*
> - *Rhubarb pie is delicious when rhubarb is in season. Cut approximately 750g rhubarb into 1cm pieces, wash and stew in a saucepan over a gentle heat until tender. Add enough sugar to taste (rhubarb needs quite a lot). Fill the pastry case with the rhubarb and cover with the pastry lid.*

🧁 PROFITEROLES 🧁

These little balls of choux pastry are remarkably easy to make but can create in impressive looking dessert that will fool your dinner guests into thinking you have slaved away over it all day. Fill the profiteroles with flavoured cream, pile high and drizzle with rich, warm chocolate or butterscotch sauce.

If you would like to make chocolate éclairs instead, then pipe the choux pastry into long fingers instead and fill with whipped cream.

Ingredients
(Makes 25)

- 115g plain flour
- Pinch of salt
- 200ml cold water
- 2tsp sugar
- 85g unsalted butter
- 3 eggs, beaten

For the filling
- 300ml whipping cream
- 1tbsp icing sugar

For the chocolate sauce
- 200g plain chocolate

- 50g butter
- 2tbsp golden syrup

Method

1. Preheat the oven to 180°C (350°F or gas mark 4) and line 2 large baking sheets with greaseproof paper or baking parchment.

2. Sift the flour and salt into a bowl and set to one side for later.

3. Place the water, sugar and butter in a large saucepan and heat over a medium heat until the butter has melted.

4. Once the mixture reaches a rolling boil, turn off the heat and put all the flour in quickly in one go.

5. Beat quickly with a wooden spoon and keep beating until the mixture turns into a thick paste and pulls away from the edges of the saucepan.

6. Tip the paste into a bowl and allow to cool for 10–15 minutes.

7. Gradually add the egg, a little at a time as you may not need it all, beating it as you go until you have a dough with a thick dropping consistency.

Pocket tip 🍪

The dough should be thick enough to hold its shape but should drop from a metal spoon when tipped.

8. Take a heaped teaspoonful at a time, place on the baking sheets and gently dab the top with a wet finger. A small spring-loaded scoop comes in very handy if you have one.

9. Place a shallow baking tray filled with water into the bottom of the oven; the steam this produces will help the pastry to puff up and create the hollow centre.

10. Bake the profiteroles for 25–30 minutes until they are crispy and golden brown. Turn off the oven.

11. Turn each profiterole over and make a little hole in the bottom with a small sharp knife then leave them on the baking tray (with the hole upwards) and put them back into the oven (still switched off) for 5 minutes.

Pocket tip 🍪

The warmth from the oven will help dry out the centres of the profiteroles and stop them from becoming soggy.

12. Remove the profiteroles from the oven and allow to cool completely on a wire rack.

13. When you are ready to fill the profiteroles, whisk the cream and icing sugar using an electric whisk until it becomes very thick.

14. Spoon the whipped cream into a piping bag and snip the end off to make a small opening. Insert the end of the piping bag into the hole in the bottom of the profiteroles and squeeze gently to fill each one.

15. To make the chocolate sauce, place the chocolate, butter and golden syrup in a heatproof bowl over a pan of gently simmering water. Stir occasionally until all the ingredients are combined and the chocolate sauce looks glossy.

16. Stack the profiteroles up in a pyramid on a pretty plate and cover with the warm chocolate sauce. Serve immediately.

Pocket fact ▬

Profiterole is a French word, although it has been used in the English language since the 16th century. It's thought that profiteroles were originally a type of pastry roll cooked in the ashes of a fire.

🧁 BAKEWELL TART 🧁

A Bakewell tart consists of a pastry case spread with jam and topped with an almond sponge mixture, and isn't to be confused with a Bakewell pudding. The tart is delicious served either warm from the oven with custard or cold, cut into slices for afternoon tea. It also makes a great lunchbox filler for both adults and children.

Ingredients

(Serves 8–10)

- 250g plain flour
- 75g white vegetable fat
- 50g baking margarine
- Water
- 1 egg white, beaten
- 2tbsp raspberry jam

For the filling

- 100g unsalted butter, softened
- 125g caster sugar
- $1/2$tsp almond extract
- 2 eggs
- 1 egg yolk
- 125g ground almonds
- 25g flaked almonds

Method

1. Sift the flour into a large bowl, dice the two types of fat and add them to the flour.

2. Rub the fat into the flour using your fingers tips or a pastry blender until it resembles fine breadcrumbs. You can also do this using a food processor.

3. Add water, a tablespoon at a time and mix it into the fat and flour. You can either use your hands or a palette knife to mix.

4. Keep adding water until the dough starts to form a ball and is soft but not sticky.

5. Roll the pastry into a ball, wrap in clingfilm and chill in the fridge for 30 minutes to 1 hour.

6. Preheat the oven to 180°C (350°F or gas mark 4) about 10–15 minutes before you are ready to bake the pastry case.

7. Lightly dust the work surface with flour then roll out the pastry into a 12 inch (30cm) circle. Place the pastry in a 9 inch (about 23cm) flan dish and gently push the pastry into the edges to mould it to the shape of the dish.

8. Trim off any excess pastry from the edges and prick the bottom of the pastry case all over with a fork

9. Line the pastry case with some greaseproof paper or baking parchment and fill with baking beans or rice.

Pocket tip 🍪

To make it easier to line the pastry case, cut a square of greaseproof paper or baking parchment and scrunch it up into a ball. Open it out and line the pastry case – it makes the paper much easier to mould to the shape.

10. Bake in the preheated oven for 20 minutes then remove the baking beans and greaseproof paper, brush the bottom of the pastry case with the beaten egg white and return to the oven for a further 3 minutes. This helps to seal the bottom of the pastry case so it doesn't become soggy.

Pocket tip 🍪

Baking beans help to stop the pastry from rising while you cook it and also help to distribute the heat evenly across the pastry. If you don't have baking beans you can use rice, dried lentils or anything dried that will weigh the pastry down.

11. Remove the pastry case from the oven and allow to cool.

12. Preheat the oven to 170°C (325°F or gas mark 3).

13. Spread the bottom of the pastry case with the jam.

14. In a large bowl cream together the butter and sugar until it's well combined then add the almond extract.

15. Lightly beat the whole eggs and extra egg yolk in a small jug then add it, along with the ground almonds, to the butter and sugar.

16. Mix until all the ingredients are well combined then pour into the pastry case.

17. Bake in the centre of the oven for 20 minutes, then scatter the flaked almonds over the top and bake for a further 15–20 minutes, until it is golden and the topping has set.

18. Allow to cool in the flan dish.

Variations to try

● To make a treacle tart filling, heat 250g of golden syrup in a saucepan until it is warm, then stir in 175g of bread-crumbs and the grated zest and juice of 1 lemon. Bake for 25–30 minutes.

Pocket fact ▬

There are several stories about the origins of the Bakewell tart but the most popular is that in 1820, the landlady of the White Horse pub, in the Derbyshire town of Bakewell, instructed her cook to make a pudding with a special egg mixture and jam spread on the top. The cook instead poured the egg and almond mixture on top of the jam, and so the Bakewell tart was born.

🧁 PLUM AND ALMOND TART 🧁

This is an incredibly easy but delicious tart. Once you have mastered the art of making puff pastry, you'll be able to experiment with different flavours and fruits in this tart, or even make individual ones. This basic pastry recipe can be used when making savoury tarts too.

Ingredients

(Serves 6–8)

- 250g plain flour
- 1/2tsp salt
- 225g butter
- 1tsp lemon juice
- 95ml cold water

For the filling

- 5 ripe plums
- 100g marzipan
- 2tsp soft light brown sugar

Method

1. You will need to make the pastry first – make sure you leave plenty of time to do this as it needs to rest for half an hour or more between each rolling.

2. Sift the flour and salt into a large bowl.

3. Mix together the lemon juice and water in a jug.

4. Dice 75g of the butter and add it to the flour. Rub it in using your fingertips or a pastry blender. You can also do this in a food processor.

5. When the mixture resembles fine breadcrumbs, start to add the water and lemon juice, a little at a time, until the dough comes together to make a ball. You may not need all the water because you want the pastry to be firm, not sticky.

6. Wrap the pastry ball in clingfilm and chill for 30 minutes in the fridge.

7. Lightly flour the work surface and roll the pastry into a rectangle measuring approximately 10 inches by 16 inches

(25cm by 40cm). Cut the remaining butter into slices and place onto two-thirds of the pastry rectangle.

8. Fold the third that isn't covered in butter over to cover third that is covered in butter, then fold the other third over the top of the other two. The butter should now be sandwiched between the pastry.

9. Turn the pastry a quarter turn and roll out by pushing the rolling pin away from you. Don't turn the rolling pin and roll the other way – the puff pastry must only be rolled in one direction at a time.

10. Fold into thirds again by folding the furthest third towards you and then the third nearest to you over the other two. Turn the pastry another quarter turn and repeat. Then fold into thirds as before, place on a plate, cover with clingfilm and chill in the fridge for 30 minutes.

11. Take the pastry out and repeat as above rolling and turning twice. Place back on the plate, cover and chill for another 30 minutes.

12. Repeat this process once more.

13. Preheat the oven to 200°C (400°F or gas mark 6) and line a baking tray with greaseproof paper or baking parchment.

14. After chilling again, remove the pastry and roll into a rectangle 14 inches by 10 inches (35cm by 25cm).

15. Trim the edges to make the rectangle 12 inches by 8 inches (30cm by 20cm) and place it onto the baking tray. Score a line around the edges to make a border that is approximately 1 inch (2.5cm wide) – this will rise and form the edge of your tart.

16. Wash and dry the plums. Cut them in half, remove the stones then cut each half into quarters.

17. Grate the marzipan and spread over the base of the tart, making sure none goes onto the border around the edge.

Pocket tip 🍪

To make it easier to grate the marzipan, freeze it for an hour before you want to use it.

18. Arrange the plums in lines on top of the marzipan, sprinkle with the sugar and bake in the centre of the oven for 20–25 minutes until the edges of pastry are risen and golden and the plums are soft.

19. Leave to cool for 5 minutes then serve warm with ice cream or cream.

Store any leftovers covered in the fridge and use the next day.

Pocket fact ▪▪▪

There are over 200 different types of plum worldwide.

CHRISTMAS BAKING

Christmas time is usually full of entertaining for family and friends and is the perfect opportunity to show off your baking skills. There are many traditional recipes to try that make your day extra special and most of them can be made well in advance, leaving you time on the day to relax a little in the knowledge that the baking is done.

🧁 MINCE PIES 🧁

It's always a good idea to have plenty of mince pies around over the Christmas season for when those unexpected visitors turn up on your doorstep or you get an impromptu invite to someone's house for drinks. You can easily make up a double batch of mince pies and freeze them, ready to defrost as and when you need them. This also means it is one less thing to rush and make on Christmas day.

While there is a huge range of ready-made mincemeat available in the supermarket, there's nothing quite the same as your own homemade. The beauty of making your own is that you can include exactly what you want and leave out anything you're not keen on. You can add brandy, rum, or apple juice for an alcohol-free version and cherries, cranberries or nuts depending on your preference.

Ingredients

(Makes 12)

- 250g plain flour
- 75g vegetable fat
- 50g butter or baking margarine

- 4–5tbsp water
- Mincemeat (see recipe on p. 114)
- Icing sugar to dust

Method

1. Sift the plain flour into a bowl then dice in the butter or baking margarine and the vegetable fat.

2. Rub the fat into the flour using your fingertips or a pastry blender. You can also do this in a food processor.

3. Add cold water, a tablespoon at a time, mixing with your fingers or a palette knife until the pastry forms a ball. Add the water slowly as you may need more or less than the recipe states. Often the temperature of the ingredients or the room can affect how much water you will need.

4. Wrap it in clingfilm and chill in the fridge of 30 minutes– 1 hour.

5. Preheat the oven to 200°C (400°F or gas mark 6) about 10–15 minutes before you plan to bake the mince pies.

6. Lightly dust the work surface with flour and roll out the pastry until it about 3mm thick. Cut out 7cm circles and press them into a bun tin.

7. Fill each pie with a heaped teaspoon of mincemeat – make sure you don't add too much or it may start to escape when you bake them!

8. Roll out the remaining pastry and either make lids for the mince pies using a slightly smaller cutter than before, or cut out stars and place them on the top of the mincemeat.

Pocket tip 🍪

If you are making lids for your mince pies, moisten around the edge of the pastry lid with a damp finger to make sure it sticks to the pastry shell underneath.

9. Brush the tops or stars with a little milk or beaten egg, make a small slit with a sharp knife in the top of each lid and bake in the centre of the oven for 20–25 minutes until the tops are golden. If you find your mince pies take longer to cook or don't turn golden, try baking them on a higher shelf or turning your oven up by 10°C.

10. Leave to cool in the tins for 5 minutes then transfer to a wire rack to cool completely.

11. Dust with icing sugar just before serving.

Store leftover mince pies in an airtight container and they will keep for several days.

Pocket fact ▬▬

The earliest type of mince pies were medieval pastries called chewettes. They were savoury pies filled with meat or chopped liver. Gradually they were enriched with dried fruits and sweet fillings until they became the mince pie we know today.

🧁 HOMEMADE MINCEMEAT 🧁

This recipe will make two 450g jars of mincemeat. Why not make a pretty fabric cover for the jar lid, tie it up with ribbon and give as a fantastic homemade Christmas gift, or as part of a homemade hamper?

Ingredients

- 100g sultanas
- 100g currants
- 150g raisins
- 100g mixed peel
- 12 glacé cherries, quartered
- Zest and juice of 1 lemon
- 2tsp mixed spice
- 1tsp ground ginger

- ¹/₂tsp ground cloves
- ¹/₂tsp nutmeg
- 1 large Bramley apple, coarsely grated
- 100ml brandy
- 175g dark muscovado sugar
- 100g shredded vegetable suet

Pocket tip 🍪

If you would prefer not to have alcohol in your mincemeat, substitute apple juice for the brandy.

Method

1. Wash all the dried fruit and glacé cherries well and place in a saucepan with the mixed peel, spices, zest and lemon juice and the grated apple.

Pocket tip 🍪

The apple will turn brown quickly once peeled so it's best to do this at the last minute.

2. Add the brandy to the fruit and heat gently for 30 minutes until the fruit has started to look plump, stirring occasionally.

3. Remove the pan from the heat and stir in the sugar, making sure you break up any large lumps before you add it.

4. Leave to cool for 20 minutes then stir in the shredded vegetable suet and spoon into sterilised jars (see p. 116), right up to the top and seal with the lids.

The unopened jars will happily keep for four months in a cool, dark place. Once opened, store the mincemeat in the fridge and use within two weeks.

How to sterilise jars

All jars need to be sterilised before you fill them with food, even if they are new jars. You can reuse old jars as long as they haven't retained a strong smell from whatever they previously contained and they have tight fitting lids. There are several ways you can sterilise jars, so choose the method that you find easiest.

Always make sure that the jars have been thoroughly cleaned before you sterilise them.

- Line a baking tray with newspaper and place the empty jars on them with the lids, inside up, next to them. Place them in the cold oven, then turn the oven on and set the temperature to 160°C (320°F or gas mark 2). Once the oven reaches this temperature, turn it off but leave the jars inside with the door still shut for 30 minutes. Remember to use oven gloves to remove them after this time as they will still be hot.
- You can also sterilise your jars using the dishwasher. Run them through on a hot wash and get them out carefully while they are still hot.
- You can also use your microwave to sterilise the jars. Clean and rinse the jars but leave them a little wet. Heat them in the microwave for no more than 1 minute.

Remember you must never add cold food to hot jars or hot food to cold jars — try to make sure the food and the jars are roughly the same temperature.

Pocket tip 🍪

If you aren't sure how many jars you will need always do more than you think will be necessary as it isn't easy to quickly sterilise more if you run out.

🧁 CHRISTMAS CAKE 🧁

No Christmas day is complete without a slice of Christmas cake and a cup of tea in the afternoon – even if you have over-indulged with the Christmas dinner! A rich, fruit-packed cake steeped in alcohol always goes down a treat so be sure to make it well before Christmas so you have time to feed it with rum or brandy.

If you aren't a big fan of alcohol or you are making a cake for the children, try soaking the fruit in apple juice, orange juice or even black tea instead.

Ingredients

(Makes an 8 inch (about 20cm) cake)

- 200g sultanas
- 225g currants
- 225g raisins
- 125g chopped mixed peel
- 100g glacé cherries, quartered
- 2tbsp brandy or rum
- 225g unsalted butter, softened
- 225g soft dark brown sugar
- 225g plain flour
- 50g ground almonds
- 1tsp ground mixed spice
- 1tsp cinnamon
- 4 eggs
- 1tbsp black treacle

Method

1. Wash the dried fruit, mixed peel and cherries and place in a bowl with the brandy or rum and leave to soak for 2 hours, or ideally overnight.

2. Preheat the oven to 140°C (275°F or gas mark 1) and line an 8 inch (20cm) round cake tin or 7 inch (18cm) square tin with greaseproof paper.

3. Sift together the flour, ground almonds and spices into a separate bowl. Take 2tbsp of the flour mixture and add it to the dried fruit, stirring well to make sure it is all coated in flour.

Pocket tip 🍪

This is an important step as coating the fruit in flour makes it much less likely to sink to the bottom as your cake cooks.

4. Cream together the butter and sugar in a large bowl until it is well combined, using a wooden spoon or in a food mixer.

5. Beat the eggs in a separate bowl with the black treacle. Add this mixture, a little at a time, to the butter and sugar, following each addition with a tablespoon of the flour.

Pocket tip 🍪

To stop the treacle sticking to your measuring spoon, heat the spoon in some boiled water first.

6. Stir well after each addition until all the egg has been added. Fold in the remaining flour with a large metal spoon.

7. Add the dried fruit to the cake mix and fold it in until it is evenly distributed.

8. Spoon the mixture into the prepared tin, even it out with the back of a spoon and make a slight hollow in the centre so it rises evenly.

9. Tie a double layer of greaseproof paper around the cake tin using string to secure it.

10. Place a tray of water in the bottom of the oven and the cake on a low shelf.

Pocket tip 🍪

Adding a tray of water to the oven will help keep the moisture in the cake, preventing it from becoming dry and cracked.

11. Bake for around $4^1/2$ hours – your oven may take longer than this. Check your cake after about 4 hours, if it's starting to look too brown on top, cover it with some greaseproof paper.

12. Test if your cake is baked through by inserting a skewer into the centre, which should come out clean.

13. Leave the cake to cool completely in the tin before turning out, keeping the greaseproof lining paper attached to the cake.

14. If you are feeding your cake, make a few holes in the top with a skewer and drizzle a couple of tablespoons of brandy or rum over it.

15. Wrap the cake in a second layer of greaseproof paper, then foil and feed every week until you are ready to add a layer of marzipan and ice it.

Variations to try

- *If you like a very boozy cake then try adding an extra 4–6 tbsp of alcohol.*
- *To add an orange twist to your Christmas cake, replace the brandy or rum with Cointreau and add the grated zest of a large orange.*
- *For a spicy cake, use ginger wine as the alcohol and add 2tsp of ground ginger.*

Pocket fact ▬

The origins of Christmas cake date way back to when it was a simple porridge eaten on Christmas Eve after a day of fasting. Gradually people started to add dried fruit, honey and spices to the porridge until it became more like the cake we know today.

🍰 CHRISTMAS PUDDING 🍰

Christmas dinner wouldn't be complete without a delicious Christmas pudding to finish off with. Wonderful served with brandy butter or cream (or both!), this pudding is packed full of fruit, and the beauty of making your own is that you can fill it with ingredients you love.

Pocket fact ▬

Christmas pudding is traditionally made on the last Sunday before Advent, which is referred to as 'Stir Up Sunday'. Everyone in the family would take it in turns to stir the pudding and make a wish.

Ingredients

(Serves 6–8)

- 115g currants
- 115g raisins
- 10 glacé cherries, quartered
- 4tbsp brandy or rum
- 1 Bramley apple, peeled, cored and grated
- 115g breadcrumbs
- 115g self-raising flour
- 115g shredded vegetable suet
- 115g dark muscovado sugar
- 1tsp mixed spice
- $^1/_2$tsp cinnamon

- 2 eggs
- Juice and finely grated zest 1 lemon
- Milk

Pocket fact -■-

The Christmas pudding is stirred from East to West in honour of the wise men who travelled to see the baby Jesus in the Nativity story.

Method

1. Wash the dried fruit and cherries and place in a bowl with the rum or brandy and leave to soak for 2 hours, or ideally overnight.

2. Grease a 2 pint (1.2 litre) pudding basin.

3. Add the chopped apple, flour, breadcrumbs, suet, sugar, mixed spice, cinnamon and grated zest and juice of the lemon to the dried fruit and stir.

Pocket fact -■-

Traditionally there were 13 ingredients in the Christmas pudding to represent Jesus Christ and his 12 disciples.

4. Lightly beat the eggs in a jug then add them to the mixture and stir again.

5. Finally add enough milk to produce a dropping consistency – the mixture shouldn't be too runny.

6. Cover the top of the bowl with a double layer of greaseproof paper and a layer of foil and tie it tightly with string.

7. Place the pudding bowl in a large saucepan, and fill the pan with boiling water until it comes to half way up the side of the pudding bowl.

8. Cover the saucepan with a lid and steam for 3 hours, topping up with more boiling water as necessary.

9. Serve warm with brandy butter or cream.

If you are making your pudding early and keeping it ready for Christmas Day, you will need to steam it again for 3 hours on the day.

Pocket fact ◄■►

It was the tradition to place a coin in the Christmas pudding when it was made in the hope that it would bring wealth to the person who found it in their pudding. Nowadays, with health and safety in mind, it isn't generally thought a good idea to place inedible objects in food — especially if children will be eating it!

🧁 CHOCOLATE YULE LOG 🧁

This squidgy chocolate log is a great alternative for those who aren't so keen on Christmas cake. It's simple to make but can be made to look very impressive with some decoration and a sprig of holly on the top.

Pocket fact ◄■►

The chocolate Yule log got its name from the log that was traditionally burned as part of the Yule, Winter Solstice and 12 Days of Christmas celebrations.

Ingredients

(Serves 8—10)

- 3 eggs
- 75g caster sugar (plus some for sprinkling)
- 60g plain flour
- 2tbsp cocoa powder
- $^1/_2$tsp baking powder

For the filling and coating

- 300ml double cream
- 225g plain chocolate
- 200g icing sugar (plus extra for dusting)

Pocket tip 🍪

Make sure the eggs are at room temperature before you start as this creates extra volume when you whisk them up.

Method

1. Preheat the oven to 180°C (350°F or gas mark 4) and line a shallow Swiss roll tin measuring approximately 12 inches by 9 inches (30cm by 23cm) with greaseproof paper or baking parchment.

2. Whisk the eggs and sugar in a large bowl with an electric whisk or in a food mixer using the whisk attachment for 7–8 minutes until the mixture is pale and has greatly increased in volume.

Pocket tip 🍪

A good test to see if you have whisked the eggs and sugar enough is to lift the whisk out of the mixture. It should leave a trail across the top of the mixture which will disappear after a few seconds.

3. Sieve the flour, cocoa powder and baking powder into the egg mixture and fold in with a large metal spoon, taking care not to knock too much air out.

4. Pour the cake batter into the prepared tin and tilt the tin backwards and forwards a few times to spread the mixture out.

5. Bake in the centre of the oven for 10–15 minutes until the sponge is set and springs back when pressed gently.

6. Place a sheet of greaseproof paper slightly larger than your sponge on the work surface and sprinkle with caster sugar.

7. Turn the sponge out onto the greaseproof paper and carefully peel away the lining paper.

8. Carefully roll up the sponge with the paper still in it and leave to cool completely.

9. To make the filling and icing for the Yule log, heat the cream in a small saucepan until it reaches boiling point.

10. Remove from the heat and break the chocolate into it. Stir quickly until it's all combined.

Pocket tip ♟

Grating the chocolate before you begin making the icing can be very handy. It makes it much easier to mix into the hot cream.

11. Beat in the sifted icing sugar until it has all been incorporated and the icing is smooth. Leave to cool completely then chill it in the fridge for an hour or so until the icing is a smooth, spreadable consistency.

12. Unroll the sponge and spread with one-third of the filling mixture. Roll it back up and place seam side down.

13. Use the rest of the filling mixture to coat the outside and ends of the Yule log. Then at about a quarter of the way down the Yule log cut off a piece at a 45° angle and stick it on one of the sides to make it look like a small branch coming off the main log.

14. Make sure all the ends are covered by the icing then use a fork to drag lines in the icing and make it look like the texture of bark.

15. Dust with icing sugar and decorate with a real or sugar paste sprig of holly.

Pocket tip ♟

If you are using a real sprig of holly make sure the berries are removed before the cake is served.

🧁 STOLLEN 🧁

This is a delicious, sweet and fruity yeast bread, with a log of marzipan running through the middle. Traditionally from Germany, it is usually eaten at Christmas time and is also known as Christstollen. Every year there is a stollen festival in Dresden, Germany when a large cake, usually weighing 3–4 tonnes, is taken through the streets on a carriage then cut with a special knife and shared amongst the crowd. The money raised goes to charity.

Pocket fact -■-

It's said that the shape of the stollen cake was supposed to represent the baby Jesus wrapped up in swaddling blankets.

Ingredients

(Makes 12–15 slices)

- 50g raisins
- 50g sultanas
- 25g mixed peel
- 10 glacé cherries, quartered
- Grated zest of 1 lemon
- $1/2$tsp nutmeg
- $1/2$tsp mixed spice
- 1tsp vanilla extract
- 350g strong white bread flour
- 50g sugar
- 7g sachet fast-action dried yeast
- Pinch of salt
- 1 egg, lightly beaten
- 50g butter, melted
- 100ml warm milk
- 200g marzipan (white is best)

Pocket tip 🍪

Add the spices to suit your taste. If you like a spicier stollen then add an extra ¹/2tsp or more of each spice.

Method

1. Wash the fruit thoroughly then place in a bowl with the mixed peel, spices, lemon zest and vanilla extract.

2. Sift the flour into a large bowl, or the bowl of your food mixer if you are using that to make your dough. Add the yeast, sugar and salt.

3. Pour in the butter, egg and warm milk and mix using a palette knife, the dough hook attachment on your food mixer or your hands.

Pocket tip 🍪

Add the milk slowly as you may not need it all. The dough should be soft but not sticky.

4. When the dough comes together in a ball, turn it out onto a lightly floured surface and knead for 10 minutes or leave in your food mixer and let it knead the dough for 5 minutes.

5. Place the dough in a lightly oiled bowl and cover with cling-film. Place the bowl in a warm, draught-free place to rise for an hour or until it has doubled in size.

6. Turn the dough out onto a floured surface and knead the fruit mix into it. Keep kneading until it is well combined.

Pocket tip 🍪

Don't be alarmed if the dough begins to get sticky. Keep going and lightly flour your hands and work surface every so often.

7. Return the dough to the oiled bowl, cover with the clingfilm and leave to rise again in a warm place for 20 minutes.

8. Dust the work surface with flour, turn out the dough and roll it into a rectangle measuring approximately 12 inches by 6 inches (30cm by 15cm).

9. Roll the marzipan into a 12 inch (30cm) long log shape and place it onto the dough.

10. Brush one of the long sides of the dough with a little milk, fold the dough over the marzipan to enclose it completely and place onto a lined baking tray with the seam underneath.

11. Cover with clingfilm and leave to rise again for 20–30 minutes.

12. Preheat the oven to 180°C (350°F or gas mark 4) 10–15 minutes before you are ready to bake the stollen.

13. Bake in the centre of the oven for 25–30 minutes until the stollen is golden and well risen.

14. Melt 1tbsp butter and brush over the top of the stollen while it's still warm.

15. Place on a wire rack to cool completely and dust generously with icing sugar before serving.

If you don't want a last minute rush to get your stollen made for Christmas, it will keep well for 3–4 days wrapped in foil or can be frozen and defrosted on the day you need it.

Variations to try

• *Try replacing some of the dried fruit in the recipe with your favourite dried fruits, such as dried apricots, dates or prunes.*

Pocket fact ▬

Like many recipes, the ingredients of stollen have changed over time. In 1427 it was made with flour, yeast, water and oil.

BAKING FOR SPECIAL OCCASIONS

No matter what the occasion, you are pretty much guaranteed that a special cake will feature highly and will probably be the centrepiece for the buffet table. Whether it's a birthday party, wedding, christening or tea on Christmas afternoon, some kind of cake is expected and this provides a fantastic opportunity for you to show off your decorating skills.

Use recipes from the other chapters in this book to make your cake and then try out some of the decoration suggestions in this chapter. Once you have mastered a few basic techniques and had a little practice, you'll soon be unleashing your creative streak and creating beautiful unique designs of your own.

🧁 BIRTHDAY CAKES 🧁

Everyone loves a good birthday cake and a homemade one tastes so much better because of the time and effort that goes into it. You can cover a simple round or square cake in sugar paste (see p. 163 for the recipe) and add decorations and a message or you can try something a bit more adventurous like baking a cake in a shaped tin or carving your own cake into a shape.

HOW TO CARVE A CAKE

When you can't quite find the right shaped tin for the cake you have in mind, you can always bake a large cake and carve it yourself.

1. Make a template of how you want the cake to look, making sure it is the actual size you want it.

2. Bake a cake that is larger than your template. You can always use the off-cuts to stick extra bits on, for example a rabbit's ears.

3. Bake your cake, wrap it in greaseproof paper and foil and leave it to rest for 24 hours. Cakes are much easier to carve once they have settled.

4. Split the cake and fill it with jam or buttercream, then put it in the freezer for an hour. This makes the crumbs hold together and it is easier to carve the cake smoothly.

5. Place your template onto the cake and carve around the shape using a sharp knife. Take your time!

6. Stick any extra cake off-cuts into place using buttercream. It may look messy now but it won't show once you decorate it.

7. Now cover your cake with sugar paste or buttercream and add the finishing touches.

TIPS FOR PIPING MESSAGES

You will usually want to pipe a message on a birthday cake for the lucky recipient but getting perfect writing can be a little tricky to begin with.

- Make sure the sugar paste has had time to dry and form a crust before you pipe your writing or designs.

- Plan where you are going to put your writing and check you have enough room before starting. It isn't easy to remove the writing without leaving a mark once you have started!

- Whilst you can pipe writing using buttercream, it's much easier to use royal icing (see p. 162 for the recipe).

- Don't overbeat your royal icing otherwise it will trap too much air. This means the tiny air bubbles come through the piping nozzle then burst, causing the line of icing to break as you pipe it.

- Use a size 1 nozzle for very fine writing and a size 2 for slightly thicker writing.

- Practise your writing on the work surface before starting. Start with your nozzle on the surface then lift it while applying an even pressure. When you need to stop, bring the tip back down onto the surface.

🧁 WEDDING CAKES 🧁

It's much easier than you might think to create a simple, stylish and elegant wedding cake and is ideal for those looking to keep to a tighter budget. Towers piled high with pretty cupcakes and a small cutting cake on top have become very popular over the past few years and are fairly simple for you to put together yourself. You can buy cupcake stands at reasonable prices or even hire one just for the day itself.

Large fruit cakes covered in marzipan and royal icing aren't as popular nowadays as they used to be but using old techniques with a modern twist can produce some stunning cakes. It doesn't have to be old fashioned sprays of sugar flowers if that's not your thing.

> *Pocket fact* ◄■■►
>
> *Wedding cakes didn't become known as such until the 19th century although the first author to describe coating a cake with marzipan and royal icing was Mrs Raffald in 1769. The cakes were referred to as 'bride cakes' or 'great cakes'.*

Stacked cakes are beginning to come back into fashion and, as long as you make a fairly firm cake, you can make different flavours for the tiers. A Madeira cake, which can be flavoured with lemon or chocolate, is a good cake as it keeps well and is firm enough to hold the icing. Unfortunately, you can't just put cakes straight on top of each other to stack them – this could end in tears as they are likely to collapse. However, with a little know-how and a few basic pieces of equipment, available from your local cake supply shop or on the internet, you can stack your own cakes too.

STACKING CAKES

You will need

- 4 plastic dowelling rods for each cake that needs stacking
- Large cake drum for the bottom cake
- Thin cake cards the same size as the cakes you are stacking

Method

1. Level all the cakes, cut off crusts, brush them with sugar syrup and fill them with jam or buttercream.

2. Place the cakes that are to be stacked on a thin cake card each and then cover them with sugar paste (p. 163) and leave them to dry overnight.

3. Make a small template to decide where your dowels will go – you will need four to support each cake. It is usually a good idea to put them at least 1 inch (2.5cm) further in than the size of the cake you are stacking.

4. Push the dowels into the cake and make a mark where they reach the top of the cake. Cut them all to the length of the longest one and reinsert them into the cake.

5. Repeat with the other tiers. Remember you won't need to put any dowels into the top tier!

6. Now you can safely stack the cakes on top of one another.

Pocket tip 🍪

If you are using cake pillars to separate the layers, make sure you mark the dowelling to the height of the top of the pillars. There will be a hole through the pillar for the dowel to go through.

You can now decorate the cake with piping, flowers or any sugar paste decorations you choose. Attach your smaller sugar paste decorations with a dab of edible glue or cooled boiled water, and your larger decorations, such as sugar flowers, with a blob of royal icing.

🧁 CHRISTENING CAKES 🧁

Decorating a christening cake is the perfect opportunity to show off your sugar modelling skills. You can easily model a pair of baby booties or a teddy bear out of gum paste or sugar paste as a stunning cake topper. Team it up with matching ribbons to go around the bottom of the cake and tie them with a big bow.

Gum paste

Gum paste is a special type of sugar dough that is ideal for modelling because it sets very hard. You can buy it from cake decorating shops, hobby shops or online in a variety of different colours. You can also use your gel or paste food colours to colour it to the exact shade you want. It is much more versatile than sugar paste because you can roll it very thin, which means it's ideal for making sugar flowers. Because it sets rock hard it also means that if you store your cake topper in a cool, dry place it will remain forever as a lasting reminder of your special day.

HOW TO MAKE GUM PASTE BABY BOOTIES

These booties will make a perfect topper to your christening cake and afterwards you can remove them and keep them in a memory box. Use pink, blue or any colour you like to add the tiny finishing touches.

1. Firstly you'll need to make a template for the sole and top of the booties – it may be a good idea to search on the internet for one or have a look at a baby bootie if you have one.

2. Roll out some gum paste to approximately 2mm thick and use your template to cut out two sole shapes.

Pocket tip 🍪

Rub some white vegetable fat onto your work surface as this stops the gum paste from sticking to it.

3. Leave the shapes to dry on a foam pad or piece of greaseproof paper.

4. Roll out the gum paste again until it's approximately 1mm thick and cut out two tops for your booties with a sharp knife.

5. Moisten the edge of the sole with edible glue then bend the top part around it so it joins at the back. Press the join together and gently press the gum paste together where the top part joins the sole.

6. Repeat for the other bootie then leave them to set hard for several hours or overnight.

7. Decorate the bootie with a small ribbon bow and a little flower.

Pocket tip 👤

Whilst gum paste is made from edible ingredients you probably don't want to eat it, especially any models you have made. It sets very hard and doesn't taste very pleasant!

🧁 EASTER CAKE 🧁

Despite the fact that simnel cake was traditionally a cake for Mothering Sunday, it has now become a popular Easter treat. A moist fruit cake is baked with a layer of marzipan in the middle, decorated with more marzipan on the top, which is then toasted in the oven to give it a golden brown colour.

Pocket fact ➖■➖

12 marzipan balls are placed on top of the cake to represent Jesus and 11 of his disciples – Judas is omitted.

Ingredients

(Serves 6–8)

- 350g dried mixed fruit
- 50g chopped mixed peel
- 75g glacé cherries, quartered
- 250g self-raising flour
- 25g ground almonds
- 1tsp ground ginger
- 1tsp ground cinnamon
- 225g butter, softened
- 225g light muscovado sugar
- 2 large eggs
- 450g white marzipan
- 1tbsp apricot jam
- Milk for brushing

Method

1. Wash the dried fruit, mixed peel and cherries, place in a large bowl and cover in hot tea (or boiling water if you don't like tea). Leave the fruit to soak for 30 minutes then drain it well or it will make the mixture soggy.

2. Preheat the oven to 140°C (275°F or gas mark 1) and line a 6 inch (about 15cm), deep round cake tin with baking parchment or greaseproof paper.

3. Sift the flour, spices and ground almonds together and mix 2tbsp in with the dried fruit. Put the rest to one side. Beat the eggs in a jug.

4. In a large bowl, cream together the butter and sugar until well combined, then gradually add the eggs and flour and mix all together.

5. Stir in the dried fruit.

6. Spoon half of the cake mixture into the prepared tin.

7. Roll out a thick layer of marzipan, cut a circle just slightly smaller than the tin, then place it on top of the cake mixture.

Spoon the rest of the cake mix on top and make a slight hollow in the centre with the back of a spoon.

8. Bake in the centre of the oven for 2 hours. If the top starts to brown too much, place some greaseproof paper over the top.

9. Leave to cool in the tin then remove it.

10. Warm the apricot jam in the microwave for a few seconds, brush it over the top and place a circle of marzipan on the top of the cake.

11. Divide the remaining marzipan into 12 balls, placing 11 around the edge and one in the centre. Fix them in place with a small dab of water. Brush the top with a little milk.

12. Preheat the oven to 180°C (350°F or gas mark 4).

13. Return the cake to the oven for 5–10 minutes to brown the marzipan but keep an eye on it so it doesn't run everywhere!

Pocket fact ◆■◆

Simnel cake started out as a cake for Mother's Day. Young girls who were working in service would make a simnel cake to take to their mother as a gift on their day off.

🧁 HALLOWEEN CAKES 🧁

Halloween has always been a popular time of year in the USA, with children (and adults) dressing up in exciting costumes, carving pumpkins, throwing parties and going trick or treating. Now it's becoming more popular in the UK too, which provides an excellent excuse for some Halloween baking!

One of the simplest things to make and decorate are some spooky cookies. The gingerbread or sugar cookie recipes in Chapter 12 are brilliant ones for decorating, and nowadays you can get a whole range of Halloween cookie cutters to help you cut out your shapes.

- Cut out pumpkin shapes and use black royal icing to make the outlines. Colour some more royal icing orange and add a little water to make a runnier consistency. Fill in the outlines with the orange icing.

- Cut out some circle shaped biscuits and pipe spider web designs using black royal icing. Pipe a spider to go in the middle or stick a jelly sweet spider onto them.

Here are some spooky ideas to jazz up some cupcakes for your Halloween party.

- Draw a bat template on a piece of paper and cut it out. Roll out some black sugar paste then use a small sharp knife to cut out bat shapes using your template. Leave them to dry then use them to decorate your cupcakes.

- Colour up some marzipan or sugar paste to a flesh colour. Shape it to look like a finger and use a cocktail stick or small knife to make the knuckle lines and fingernail shapes. Paint a little red food colouring on to look like blood then stick the fingers in the top of your cupcakes.

- Roll a small oblong of marzipan or sugar paste and sit it on top of your cupcakes. Drape some white sugar paste over the top and attach two black eyes and open mouth to look like a ghost.

Pocket fact ◄■►

The colours orange and black that are associated with Halloween are thought to have stemmed from the orange colours associated with the harvest and black for death.

BAKING WITH CHILDREN

It's great to get children involved in the kitchen from an early age and there are lots of jobs they can do to help. A little apron and a children's baking kit can really spark their imagination and before you know it, they will be creating masterpieces to be proud of. Put on your aprons together, forget about the mess and get stuck in!

Whilst you can bake almost any recipe together, there are some that are particularly great for children. Most of these are brilliant because not only can they help bake the goodies, but because there is lots of decoration involved. Children love to get their hands on sprinkles, silver balls and jelly tots, but don't expect them to last long – the saying 'less is more' doesn't enter into their vocabulary!

Many of these recipes are also fantastic for creating treats to serve at birthday parties or when the children have their friends round for tea.

🧁 GINGERBREAD MEN 🧁

Gingerbread men will always be a favourite family recipe because they are such fun to cut out and decorate. Play with the recipe and adjust the amount of ginger until it suits your tiny tots' taste buds. Once you've got the recipe under your belt you can get a set of cookie cutters and branch out into making many different shapes – they also make great Christmas presents for the grandparents or pretty Christmas tree decorations.

Pocket fact -■-

Gingerbread dates as far back as the 15th century. Gingerbread figures started to appear during the 16th century.

Ingredients

(Makes about 12 — depending on the size of your cutter)

- 350g plain flour
- 115g unsalted butter
- 1tsp bicarbonate of soda
- 2tsp ground ginger
- 175g light soft brown sugar
- 1 egg
- 4tbsp golden syrup

Method

1. Preheat the oven to 190°C (375°F or gas mark 5) and lightly grease 3 large baking sheets. If you can't fit all 3 sheets in at once, you can bake the gingerbread men in batches.

2. Rub together the butter, flour, bicarbonate of soda and ginger either by hand or using a food processor, until it resembles fine breadcrumbs.

Pocket tip 🍪

Add enough ginger to suit your taste. If you like spicier ginger-bread then add extra teaspoons.

3. Mix in the sugar.

4. In a separate bowl whisk together the egg and golden syrup.

5. Add the egg and syrup mixture to the flour and butter mixture to form a dough. Either mix together with a wooden spoon or continue to use the food processor.

Pocket tip 🎄

Add the egg and syrup mixture slowly as you may not need the full amount. Adding too much liquid will make the dough sticky and difficult to work with.

6. Turn out the dough onto a lightly floured surface and knead for about 30 seconds just to bring it all together into a smooth ball.

7. Roll the dough out to about 3mm thick and cut out your shapes. Gather up the remaining dough and repeat until you have used it all up.

8. Place the gingerbread men onto the lightly greased baking sheets, leaving space between them to allow for spreading.

9. Bake for approximately 12–15 minutes, until they are golden brown in colour.

10. Leave to cool on the trays for 2 minutes then carefully remove them to a wire rack to cool.

Pocket fact ➖

Gingerbread is also used to construct edible houses, especially at Christmas time, because it holds its shape well and is firm enough to stand upright.

Once the gingerbread is completely cool you are ready to decorate with whatever you fancy. Raisins are great for adding eyes, and jelly tots, or Smarties make colourful buttons. Royal icing (p. 162) is good for attaching the sweets and you can buy handy ready-made tubes of icing from the supermarket – simple and brilliant for little hands.

Pocket fact ◄■►

According to the Guinness Book of Records, *the world's largest gingerbread man was made by the Smithville Area Chamber of Commerce in Texas for their Festival of Lights celebration in December 2006. It stood over 20ft (about 6 metres) high and weighed 1,308lb, 8oz (about 600kg).*

🧁 FAIRY CAKES 🧁

A fairy cake is the cupcake's little sister. They are baked in smaller cases and are ideal for little teatime or lunch box treats. You can buy all sorts of pretty fairy cake cases and children love decorating them with all manner of toppings.

Ingredients

(Makes 12)

- 85g baking margarine
- 85g caster sugar
- 85g self-raising flour
- $^1/_2$tsp baking powder
- $^1/_2$tsp vanilla extract
- 1 large egg

Method

1. Preheat the oven to 170°C (325°F or gas mark 3) and place 12 fairy cake cases in the wells of a 12 hole bun tin.

2. Cream together the baking margarine and caster sugar until soft and fluffy, either with a wooden spoon or a food mixer.

3. Sift together the flour and baking powder.

4. Add the egg and vanilla extract to the margarine and sugar mix, along with 1tbsp of the flour. Beat until combined.

5. Fold in the rest of the flour with a metal spoon or mix on a slow speed in the food mixer.

6. Divide the mixture between the 12 cake cases, making sure they aren't more than three-quarters full.

7. Bake for 10–15 minutes until the cakes are golden and risen, and spring back when pressed gently in the centre with a clean finger.

8. Leave the cakes to cool for 5 minutes in the tin and then remove to a wire rack to cool completely.

DECORATION IDEAS

- The best decoration for fairy cakes is some simple glacé icing. Mix together 100g sieved icing sugar with approximately 15ml of cold water and mix to a smooth paste.

Pocket tip 🍪

If the icing is too stiff add more water, a drop at a time, until you reach the correct consistency. If it is too runny, add some more sieved icing sugar, a tablespoon at a time.

- Spread onto the cakes and decorate with sprinkles, silver balls, icing flowers, jelly tots, chocolate beans, glacé cherries or whatever takes the children's fancy. There are many different decorations available in the supermarkets, with some great ones especially for children.

- You can also get children to make their own fairy cake decorations by rolling out some coloured sugar paste and letting them cut out various shapes with cutters. Plunger cutters are excellent for children as the shapes are easily released from the cutters by pushing the plungers. You can get all sorts of shapes including stars, flowers, snowflakes and holly leaves.

Variations to try

- *To make lovely little butterfly cakes, cut a small circle out of the top of the cake with a sharp knife and fill the hole with buttercream. Cut the circle in half and press the two halves into the buttercream at an angle to look like wings. Dust with icing sugar.*
- *Flavour the glacé icing by replacing some of the water with the juice from an orange. Decorate the cakes with jelly orange and lemon slices.*
- *Make chocolate fairy cakes by replacing 10g of the flour with 10g of cocoa powder. Make some chocolate icing by mixing 2tsp of cocoa powder with 4tsp of boiling water and adding to the icing sugar. Add more water if necessary to make into a spreadable consistency. Decorate with coloured chocolate beans or white chocolate buttons.*

🧁 SMARTIE COOKIES 🧁

These cookies are really easy to whip up quickly and always go down a storm. They are a great addition to a lunchbox, or an after-school treat with a nice cold glass of milk. It is also a great recipe to involve children with, especially choosing what colour Smarties to put on each cookie!

Ingredients

(Makes 12 cookies)

- 125g unsalted butter, softened
- 100g soft light brown sugar
- 1tsp vanilla extract
- 2tbsp golden syrup
- 150g plain flour
- $^1/_2$tsp baking powder
- 2 tubes of Smarties

Method

1. Preheat the oven to 180°C (350°F or gas mark 4). Grease and line 2 large baking sheets with parchment paper.

2. Cream together the butter and sugar in a bowl until it's soft and well combined using a wooden spoon or food mixer.

3. Add the vanilla extract and golden syrup and mix again.

4. Sift in the flour and baking powder and mix together to form a soft dough.

Pocket tip 🍪

It may be easier to bring the ingredients together to form a dough using your hands. Children love to get stuck in helping with this!

5. Divide the mixture into 12 equal balls. A spring-loaded scoop can be very useful to help you do this.

6. Place the dough balls onto the prepared baking sheets, leaving plenty of room between them as the cookies will spread as they bake.

7. Press 5 or 6 Smarties into each dough ball, but don't flatten the cookies. It may look like the Smarties are very close together but don't worry, they will spread out as the cookies are in the oven.

8. Bake for around 15–20 minutes until the cookies have become flatter and golden.

9. Leave the cookies to cool on the trays for 5 minutes and then remove them to a wire rack to cool completely.

Stored in an airtight container, they will last for a few days – or maybe not depending on your children!

Variations to try

- You can experiment with other types of sweet to see what works well.
- Press chocolate chips or chunks into the cookie dough instead of Smarties – white chocolate works very well.
- Mix a handful of raisins or dried cranberries in with the dough to make fruity cookies. Maybe add a few chocolate chunks too!
- For fudgy cookies, press small pieces of fudge into the cookie dough before baking. You can often buy bags of fudge chunks in the baking section at the supermarket or buy a pack of fudge pieces and chop them up with a sharp knife.

🧁 RICE KRISPIES CAKES 🧁

This is such a quick and simple recipe that even tiny tots can help out. They can easily get involved with the measuring, setting the cake cases out, breaking the chocolate and stirring in the Rice Krispies. It's also an ideal after-school activity with older children and it means you have an after-dinner snack all ready for them!

Ingredients

(Makes 12 large or 15 smaller cakes)

- 50g butter
- 100g milk chocolate
- 3tbsp golden syrup
- 85g Rice Krispies

Method

1. Set out 12 fairy cake cases in the wells of a 12 hole bun tin.

2. Break the chocolate into squares and place in a fairly large saucepan with the butter and golden syrup.

Pocket tip 🍪

To stop the golden syrup sticking to the spoon so much, gently warm the spoon for 5 seconds or so over the hob. Be careful not to burn your fingers, especially if you are cooking with children!

3. Melt the ingredients together over a gentle heat, stirring occasionally.

4. When everything is melted, remove from the heat and stir in the Rice Krispies.

5. Use 2 teaspoons (one to scoop the mixture and one to push it off the spoon) to spoon equal amounts into each cake case.

6. Leave to set. You can also refrigerate them, which will help the mixture to stick together better.

These cakes will keep for a day or two in an airtight container, preferably in the fridge.

Variations to try

- *For something a little bit special try adding a handful of marshmallows.*
- *To give the Rice Krispies cakes a fruity twist add a handful of raisins and 10 glacé cherries, cut into quarters.*
- *Children aren't always fans of dark chocolate but try using different kinds of chocolate. White chocolate is often a big hit with kids.*

🧁 SUGAR COOKIES 🧁

These cookies are great to bake with younger children because they need to be baked and decorated in three stages – ideal for short attention spans! They are also so easy to whip up from just a few basic store cupboard ingredients.

Sugar cookies are ideal to decorate with sugar paste cut-outs or even royal icing. Older children can be particularly creative with them and bake gifts for family members or friends. Tie the cookies up in a cellophane bag with some pretty ribbons and everyone will be impressed.

Ingredients

(Makes 15–18)

- 200g unsalted butter, softened
- 225g caster sugar
- 1 egg
- 1tsp vanilla extract
- 400g plain flour

Method

1. Cream together the butter, sugar and vanilla extract in a mixing bowl until it is light and fluffy. You can either use a wooden spoon or a food mixer.

Pocket tip 🍪

If you are getting the children to cream the ingredients together, make sure the butter is well softened to make it easier for them. Blast it for 20–30 seconds in a microwave on a medium heat to soften it.

2. Add the egg and 1tbsp of flour to the butter and sugar in a bowl and mix until all the egg has been incorporated.

3. Sift in the flour and mix until you have a soft dough. Younger children might need some help mixing as the dough starts to form because it can be quite tiring for little hands.

4. Once you have your dough mixed, make it into a ball, wrap tightly in clingfilm and chill in the fridge for an hour. It will happily stay in the fridge longer than that until you need it.

5. When you are ready to make your cookies, preheat the oven to 180°C (350°F or gas mark 4) and line 2 baking sheets with greaseproof paper or baking parchment.

6. Lightly flour the work surface and roll out the dough until it's approximately 3mm thick.

7. Cut out shapes using cookie cutters and place them on the lined baking sheets.

Pocket tip 🍪

If you are cutting out lots of different sized cookies, try to place similar sized cookies on the same baking sheet. This means they will all cook at the same rate and the small ones won't get burnt while the larger ones are still cooking.

---

8. Bake in the centre of the preheated oven for 10–12 minutes until the cookies are starting to turn golden brown.

9. Leave to cool on the baking trays for a few minutes then remove to wire racks to cool completely before decorating.

Un-iced, the cookies will last well for a couple of weeks when wrapped in foil or stored in an airtight container.

Variations to try

- *To make pretty Christmas tree decorations, cut out star, snowflake or bauble shapes from the cookie dough and make a small hole with a skewer at the top before baking. Once they are cool decorate using some of the ideas below and thread a ribbon through each hole.*

- *To make lollipop sugar cookies, cut out circles from the dough and insert a lolly stick (available from cake decorating shops, craft shops such as HobbyCraft and online) into the cookie before baking. Decorate using the ideas below then tie up the cookie in pretty cellophane with ribbons. These make brilliant party bag fillers and you can pipe each child's name on them too (see p. 129 for tips on piping writing).*

DECORATION IDEAS

- Roll out coloured sugar paste (p. 163) and use the same cookie cutters you used to cut out your cookies to cut out matching shapes. Mix up a batch of royal icing (p. 162). Spread a small amount of royal icing onto the top of the cookie and lay the matching cut-out sugar paste shape on the top. Leave to dry then pipe additional details with the remaining royal icing.

- Mix up a batch of royal icing thick enough for piping. Fit a size 2 nozzle to your piping bag and fill with the royal icing. Carefully pipe all around the edge of the cookie.

Pocket tip 🍪

When piping around the cookie start a millimetre or so in from the edge; if you go too close to the edge you will find it tricky to keep the line from dropping off the side.

Then take some of the remaining icing and add a teaspoon of water to thin it down until it spreads when you test drop a teaspoonful onto the work surface. Place the thinned icing in a piping bag, cut off the tip to make an opening of 1–2mm then flood the inside of the cookie with the icing, spreading it with the tip of the piping bag as you go. You can pipe lines inside the cookie too and use different coloured icing to make patterns and designs.

- If you are decorating the cookies with very young children just mix up some simple glacé icing to spread on the cookie and let them decorate the cookies with sprinkles, silver balls and sweets.

Pocket fact ━■━

The Commonwealth of Pennsylvania adopted the sugar cookie as their official cookie in September 2001.

ALLERGY-FRIENDLY BAKING

Nowadays people are more aware of their food allergies and intolerances, and with such a huge range of products available in the supermarkets and health food shops, they needn't miss out on baked treats. You can buy different kinds of flours, many of them gluten-free, egg substitutes and dairy-free spreads, meaning you can still bake delicious treats for people with allergies. You can also use other everyday items as substitutes, such as ground almonds in place of flour and oil instead of eggs.

🧁 FLOURLESS CHOCOLATE 🧁 BROWNIES

As long as you check the ingredients in your chocolate, these delicious, chocolatey brownies are ideal for those following a gluten-free diet. Ground almonds are used in place of flour in this recipe making it incredibly moist and moreish.

The brownies are gorgeous served warm from the oven with cream or ice cream or leave them to cool completely and eat them for tea.

Ingredients

(Makes 16 squares)

- 200g plain chocolate, at least 70% solids
- 200g unsalted butter
- 1tsp vanilla extract
- 150g caster sugar
- 150g ground almonds
- 3 eggs, lightly beaten

Method

1. Preheat the oven to 170°C (325°F or gas mark 3) and line a 9 inch (24cm) square baking tin with baking parchment or greaseproof paper.

2. Break the chocolate into a medium-sized saucepan and add the butter. Gently heat until they have melted and combined, stirring occasionally.

3. Remove the saucepan from the heat and stir in the vanilla extract and caster sugar.

4. Leave to cool for 5 minutes then stir in the ground almonds followed by the beaten eggs. Mix well to combine.

5. Pour the mixture into the prepared tin and bake in the centre of the oven for 25–30 minutes until the brownie has set.

6. Leave to cool completely in the tin then cut into pieces and remove.

The brownies will keep for 2–3 days stored in an airtight container.

Pocket fact -■-

It is estimated that around 10%–15% of people have a gluten intolerance, although many suffer such mild symptoms they don't realise they have it.

🧁 EGGLESS COFFEE CAKE 🧁

This is a super, moist cake that is both egg- and dairy-free. The mixture of oil and water in this recipe replaces the eggs and adding some coffee granules to the water gives it a lovely flavour. It's also really quick to mix up and will keep well in an airtight container for 2–3 days.

Ingredients

(Serves 10–12)

- 225g self-raising flour
- 2tsp baking powder
- 175g caster sugar
- 100ml sunflower oil
- 200ml water
- 1tbsp instant coffee granules

Method

1. Preheat the oven to 170°C (325°F or gas mark 3) and line a deep 7 inch (18cm) round baking tin with greaseproof paper or baking parchment.

2. Sift the flour and baking powder into a large mixing bowl and stir in the sugar.

3. Place the instant coffee granules into a small measuring jug and pour over 2tbsp of boiling water. Mix until they have dissolved then top it up to the 200ml mark with cold water.

Pocket tip 🍪

If you like your coffee strong, try adding more instant coffee granules to suit your taste.

4. Make a well in the centre of the flour and add the coffee mix and the sunflower oil.

5. Stir with a wooden spoon or large balloon whisk to combine.

6. Pour into the tin and bake in the centre of the oven for 45–50 minutes until the cake is risen and a skewer inserted into the centre comes out clean.

Pocket tip 🍪

Don't open the door of the oven to check the cake too soon as the rush of cold air will stop the cake from rising.

7. Allow the cake to cool in the tin for 20 minutes before removing it to a wire rack to cool completely.

Variations to try

- *This cake will also work well as a plain vanilla sponge cake. Leave out the coffee granules and add 2tsp vanilla extract instead.*
- *For a chocolate cake replace 25g of the flour with sifted cocoa powder.*

Pocket fact ━■━

Egg allergy is the second most common food allergy in children after cow's milk allergy.

🧁 GLUTEN-FREE BREAD 🧁

Bread can be one of the hardest things to substitute when you are on a gluten-free diet. It can be very expensive to buy in the supermarkets but with some practice and tweaking the recipe to suit your taste, you can be baking fresh, tasty gluten-free bread in no time.

Nowadays you can get handy packets of gluten-free bread flour that contain ingredients such as xanthan gum already added for you. The Doves Farm brand is especially good and can be bought in most supermarkets or health food stores.

Ingredients

(Makes a 1lb loaf)

- 450g gluten-free white bread flour (such as Doves Farm)
- 1tsp salt
- 2tsp fast-action dried yeast
- 1tsp caster sugar

- 300ml milk
- 1tsp white vinegar
- 2 eggs
- 75ml sunflower oil

Method

1. Sift the flour into a large bowl and stir in the salt, yeast and sugar.

2. In a jug mix together the milk, vinegar and eggs.

3. Make a well in the centre of the flour mix and pour in the wet ingredients. Mix well to combine – the dough will be quite sticky.

4. Pour the oil over the dough and bring it together into a ball.

5. Place the dough into a 1lb loaf tin, cover with clingfilm and leave in a warm, draught-free area to rise for an hour.

6. Preheat the oven to 200°C (400°F or gas mark 6) 15 minutes before you plan to bake the loaf.

7. Place the loaf tin in the centre of the preheated oven and bake for 30–35 minutes until the loaf is risen and the crust is a golden brown colour.

8. Leave to cool in the tin for 10 minutes then transfer to a wire rack to cool completely.

🧁 MERINGUES 🧁

Meringue is made from egg whites and sugar so it is naturally gluten-free. You can use a basic meringue mix to make all sorts of different treats. Try using food colours to make pretty mini-meringues or make one large one and fill it with cream and fresh fruit for a delicious dessert.

Pocket fact ▬

A popular meringue-based dessert is the pavlova, which was named after the famous Russian ballerina Anna Pavlova, to honour her visit to Australia and New Zealand in the 1920s.

Ingredients

(Makes 12)

- 4 egg whites
- 200g caster sugar

Pocket tip 🍪

For every egg white that you use, you should add 50g of caster sugar.

Method

1. Make sure all the equipment you are using is very clean and grease-free. Even the smallest speck of grease can prevent the egg whites from whisking up properly.

2. Preheat the oven to 140°C (275°F or gas mark 1) and line 2 large baking sheets with greaseproof paper or baking parchment.

3. Crack the egg whites into a large bowl, making sure that no yolk gets in there at all, otherwise the whites won't whisk well.

4. With an electric whisk, begin to whisk the eggs at a slow speed. Do this for about 2–3 minutes until the eggs begin to get frothy.

Pocket tip 🍪

It's best to use really fresh eggs when making meringues.

5. Turn the whisk up to a slightly higher speed for 1 minute, then up to the fastest speed until the eggs form stiff peaks. You can test this by lifting the whisk out to see if the peaks stand up without falling from the whisk. Don't over-whisk them or they will begin to form a liquid again.

Pocket tip 🍪

If you are feeling brave, you can test if the egg whites have been whisked enough by holding the bowl upside down over your head!

6. Keeping the whisk on a fast speed, begin to add the sugar about 1tbsp at a time until it has all been incorporated and the mixture looks glossy.

7. Spoon the mixture onto the prepared sheets a tablespoonful at a time. It doesn't matter if they look a bit rustic, that is one of the charms of homemade meringues.

8. Bake the meringues for 45–60 minutes until they look crisp but haven't taken on much colour, then turn off the oven but leave them in until it is cold.

9. Remove the meringues from the baking sheets and serve.

You can either fill or sandwich the meringues together with cream, dip them in melted chocolate or eat them as they are. Store them in an airtight container and they will keep well for a week.

🧁 DAIRY- AND GLUTEN-FREE 🧁 VANILLA CUPCAKES

These vanilla cupcakes are brilliant because they are suitable for those with gluten and dairy allergies but don't fall short in taste. They are made using rice flour, which is a great substitute for regular flour.

Pocket tip 🍪

If you are using baking powder in your gluten-free baking, make sure you check the label as not all baking powder is suitable for people with a gluten allergy.

Ingredients

(Makes 12)

- 125g dairy-free margarine
- 125g caster sugar
- 125g rice flour
- 1tsp gluten-free baking powder
- 2 eggs
- 1tsp gluten-free vanilla extract

Method

1. Preheat the oven to 170°C (325°F or gas mark 3) and place paper cupcake cases in the wells of a 12 hole muffin tin.

2. In a large bowl or your food mixer, cream together the dairy-free margarine and sugar until well combined and fluffy.

3. Sift the flour and baking powder into a separate bowl.

4. Add the vanilla extract, one of the eggs and 1tbsp of flour to the margarine and sugar mixture and beat until it has been combined.

5. Add the second egg and 1tbsp of flour again and mix together.

6. Finally, fold in the remaining flour with a large metal spoon.

7. Divide the cake batter equally between the 12 cupcake cases and bake in the centre of the preheated oven for 20–25 minutes until the cakes are golden brown.

8. Leave to cool in the tin for 5 minutes then transfer to a wire rack to cool completely before decorating.

You can either decorate the cupcakes with a simple glacé icing or try out this dairy-free buttercream recipe.

DAIRY-FREE BUTTERCREAM

There is actually quite a large range of dairy-free margarines on sale now and not all of them will behave in the same way when you are making buttercream. Experiment with this recipe, perhaps adding the icing sugar slowly, until you get the flavour and consistency you like.

Ingredients

(Makes enough to decorate 12 or more cupcakes)

- 100g dairy-free margarine
- 250g icing sugar
- $^1/_2$tsp vanilla extract
- A little soy milk or water

Method

1. Place the dairy-free margarine in a large bowl and add half the icing sugar. Beat together until well combined. Add the rest of the icing sugar and beat again.

2. Add the vanilla extract and a little soy milk or water if you feel the icing needs it. Beat again until it's all combined and the consistency you want.

3. Pipe or spread the icing onto the cupcakes and decorate.

🧁 SUGAR-FREE GINGER BISCUITS 🧁

You can often replace the sugar in recipes with honey or sugar-free jam. Not only is this great for those who have to watch the amount of sugar they eat but it's also brilliant for children when you are trying to limit their intake of sugary foods.

Pocket tip 🍪

Remember that children under the age of 12 months should not be given honey as it can be harmful for them.

Ingredients

(Makes 12)

- 75g unsalted butter
- 2tbsp runny honey
- 250g plain flour
- Pinch of salt
- $^1/_2$tsp baking powder

- 1tsp ground ginger
- 1 egg

Method

1. Preheat the oven to 180°C (350°F or gas mark 4) and grease a large baking tray.

2. Melt the honey and butter together over a gentle heat in a medium-sized saucepan.

3. Leave to cool for 5 minutes.

4. Sift together the flour, salt, baking powder and ground ginger into a large bowl.

5. Lightly beat the egg with a fork or whisk in a small jug.

6. Stir the flour mixture and beaten egg into the melted butter and honey until it forms a soft dough.

7. Roll into a ball then place on a lightly floured work surface.

8. Using a non-stick rolling pin, roll out the biscuit dough until it is approximately 3mm thick. Cut out shapes using cookie cutters and place onto the prepared baking tray.

9. Bake in the centre of the oven for 10–12 minutes until the biscuits are golden brown.

10. Leave them to cool on the tray for a couple of minutes then transfer them to a wire rack to cool.

Variations to try

- *Experiment using different spices. Make spiced biscuits by replacing the ginger with 1tsp ground mixed spice and $^1/_2$tsp cinnamon.*

- *To make oat biscuits, replace 100g of the flour with rolled oats and add a handful of washed sultanas.*

Pocket fact -■-

More children than adults suffer from a milk allergy and many of those children outgrow the allergy by the age of three.

DECORATION AND PRESENTATION

Cake decorating is fast becoming a popular hobby and there are so many wonderful ideas in a wealth of books and on the internet for making your baked creations look stunning. You can buy sprinkles and cake decorations galore in high street shops and dozens of online stores, and even the supermarkets are increasing their stocks in the baking section.

However, you don't have to stick to shop-bought decorations. Once you have mastered a few simple techniques for working with buttercream, sugar paste and flower paste, you'll soon be letting your imagination run wild and creating your own unique masterpieces.

🧁 TYPES OF ICING 🧁

BUTTERCREAM

The most popular choice for icing cupcakes is buttercream, often piled high in big swirls. It can be coloured to create pretty effects and is also an excellent choice for filling and topping large cakes.

Simple buttercream

This is a simple recipe with few ingredients but it creates a delicious topping or filling for your cakes.

Pocket tip 🧍

If you have a food mixer it's a good idea to use it to make buttercream. It is possible to make the icing by hand but it's quite a hard task!

Ingredients

(Makes enough to ice about 24 cupcakes)

- 250g butter, softened
- 500g icing sugar, sifted
- 1–2tbsp milk
- 1tsp vanilla extract

Method

1. Make sure your butter is at room temperature before you start, especially if you are making the buttercream by hand.

2. Beat the butter until it is pale and fluffy.

Pocket tip 🍪

The longer you beat the butter, the whiter it will become. However it will never be completely white because of the colour of the butter to begin with.

3. Sift in half of the icing sugar and beat well for a couple of minutes to combine. Use a splash guard on your mixer if you have one – icing sugar gets everywhere!

4. Add the other half of your icing sugar and beat well again until it is all combined.

5. Add 1–2tbsp of milk and the vanilla extract and beat for another 2 minutes until the buttercream is a soft consistency. If you are colouring your buttercream, add the food colouring now (see the box on p. 164).

Pocket tip 🍪

Practice makes perfect when it comes to knowing how much milk to add. The weather can also affect how the buttercream behaves. For example, on a hot day you may not need to add any milk at all.

6. Spread or pipe the buttercream onto your cupcakes.

Pocket tip 🍪

To make chocolate buttercream add 2tbsps of cocoa powder to your icing sugar. You can adjust the amount of cocoa powder to suit your taste, or you can make a luxurious chocolate buttercream by melting chocolate and adding it to your buttercream — again you can add as much as you like according to your preferences.

ROYAL ICING

Royal icing is made from icing sugar, egg whites and lemon juice and dries to make a hard white icing. You can use it to cover marzipanned fruit cakes and to pipe writing, different patterns and designs. You can also use professional liquid food colours to colour the icing. Adding a little glycerine to the royal icing when you make it up prevents it from setting quite so hard and makes it easier to cut without it shattering. Traditionally, royal icing is used to decorate Christmas and wedding cakes, although now sugar paste is becoming much more popular too.

Pocket tip 🍪

You should only use liquid food colours to colour royal icing as paste colours contain glucose or glycerine, which softens the icing too much.

It's easy to make up your own batches of royal icing and although it is possible to do it by hand, it is much easier to use a food mixer to make it because it requires a great deal of beating. You can also buy packets of royal icing powder in the supermarkets or cake decorating shops, to which you just need to add a little water and beat in a food mixer for around 10–12 minutes.

It is preferable to use dried egg albumen when making up royal icing but you can use fresh egg whites too. If using dried albumen you need to mix it with water the night before to reconstitute it and if you are using fresh egg whites then you need to separate them the night before and add either 5–7 drops of lemon juice or 4–5 drops of white vinegar to them.

Making royal icing using fresh eggs

Ingredients

- 3 fresh egg whites
- 450g icing sugar
- 5–7 drops lemon juice or 4–5 drops white vinegar

Method

1. Separate the egg whites the day before you plan to use them and store them, covered, in the fridge. Pass them through a sieve the next day.

2. Place the egg whites in a bowl, add the lemon juice or vinegar and sift in the icing sugar. Beat until it is well combined (around 10–12 minutes in a food mixer) and has reached the stage where it will form stiff peaks.

3. Cover with a damp cloth to prevent the icing from drying out when you aren't using it.

Pocket tip 🧍

See p. 141 for tips on how to make glacé icing.

🧁 SUGAR PASTE 🧁

Sugar paste is a mixture of icing sugar, water and gum tragacanth, which is mixed together until it forms a thick paste. It's generally used to cover cakes and cupcakes as it can be rolled out and takes to the shape of the cake you are covering without cracking or breaking. You can also colour it using paste food colours and mould it into different shapes, which harden when left to dry.

You will find a range of sugar paste available in the supermarkets now, often called 'ready to roll' icing. In some cases you can get it ready rolled too. This is great to keep in your store cupboard and is ideal for covering small cakes and making decorations from. If you are going to be covering a large cake or a cake for a special occasion, it's a good idea to buy professional-quality sugar paste from a cake-decorating supply shop or online store. It is easier to work with and will give you the lovely smooth finish you're looking for.

Colouring buttercream and sugar paste

It's best to avoid the cheap liquid food colouring to colour your icing as you need to add quite a lot to get a strong colour and it will change the consistency. Gel and paste food colours do the job much more effectively; you need to use much less so they last a long time, making them good value for money too. You can also buy professional liquid food colouring, which is much more concentrated than the supermarket kind, so you only need a few drops to colour your icing. Often the gel and paste colours intensify after you have added them so leave the buttercream for a while to check you have got the colour you want.

Pocket tip 🍪

Add food colouring a small amount at a time, using a cocktail stick. You can always add more but it isn't that easy to take away once you've added it!

COVERING A CAKE IN SUGAR PASTE

The first time you roll out your sugar paste to cover a cake it can be quite daunting, but rest assured, practice does make perfect. Remember to take your time and have all the equipment out and ready, near you before you begin.

If you are covering a cake in sugar paste, make sure it is able to take the weight. Fruit or Madeira cakes are ideal as they have a firm texture.

Equipment

- Cake board
- Non-stick rolling pin
- Cake smoother
- Clingfilm
- Sharp knife

1. Check you have enough sugar paste to cover the cake you have made. Often the packet will give you a guideline for different cake sizes but as a rough guide you will need at least:

Round cake	Sugar paste	Square cake	Sugar paste
6 inches	500g	6 inches	500g
7 inches	500g	7 inches	750g
8 inches	750g	8 inches	1kg
9 inches	1kg	9 inches	1.25kg
10 inches	1.25kg	10 inches	1.5kg

2. Prepare your cake and place it on a cake board.

Pocket tip 🍪

It's best to choose a cake board that is at least 2 inches bigger than your cake. You can roll out some sugar paste and cover the board, sticking it down with some boiled water first if you want to.

3. If the cake is already covered in marzipan then you will need to brush it with a little alcohol, such as gin or vodka, or plain boiled water before you cover it in sugar paste. If it is a Madeira cake then you will need to apply a thin layer of buttercream first.

4. Knead the sugar paste until it is soft and pliable. Add the food colour if you need to.

Pocket tip 🍪

Make sure you colour enough sugar paste to cover the whole cake and for any other matching decorations. It's almost impossible to mix up exactly the same colour again!

5. Dust the work surface with icing sugar. Don't use cornflour, especially if you are covering a marzipanned cake, as it can ferment under certain conditions.

6. Roll the sugar paste wide enough to cover the cake. Remember to measure the depth of the sides as well, so for an 8 inch (20cm) cake that is 3 inches (8cm) deep you will need to make sure the sugar paste is at least 14 inches by 14 inches (36cm by 36 cm).

Pocket tip 🍪

You want to avoid getting any icing sugar on the surface of the sugar paste as this will make it dry out and crack. Using a non-stick rolling pin will help.

7. Place your rolling pin gently in the centre of the sugar paste and fold the back part towards you over the rolling pin.

8. Lift up the rolling pin and gently lay the sugar paste over the cake so that the rolling pin is over the centre point of the cake.

9. Make sure your hands are free from icing sugar then gently lift the edges of the sugar paste and push them towards the sides of the cake. Once they are in place press them with your hand to make sure they are firmly stuck to the sides of the cake.

10. Use a cake smoother or a small ball of sugar paste wrapped in clingfilm to smooth the top and edges.

11. Using a sharp knife, trim the excess sugar paste from the bottom of the cake.

12. It's best to leave the cake overnight so that the sugar paste will harden a little before you add any decoration.

Pocket fact ▰

During the 16th and 17th centuries sugar paste models were used to decorate banqueting tables.

🧁 SUGAR PASTE DECORATIONS 🧁

It's very easy to make your own sugar paste decorations to decorate your cakes and cupcakes using some coloured sugar paste and different shaped cutters. You'll find a whole range of cutters at your local cake supply shop, craft shops such as HobbyCraft and on the internet. Have a look at p. 11 for a list of good websites selling cake-decorating equipment. The plunger cutters are especially useful as they push the sugar paste out for you once you have cut it, sometimes adding shapes or markings into the design too, for example the butterfly cutters often emboss patterns onto the wings.

To make your own decorations:

1. Colour the sugar paste to the colours you will need, keeping the ones you aren't using wrapped in clingfilm to prevent them from drying out.

2. Lightly dust the work surface with icing sugar, then roll out your first piece of sugar paste using a small non-stick rolling pin until it is about 2mm thick.

3. Cut out shapes using your cutters and place them onto a foam pad or piece of greaseproof paper to dry out.

Pocket tip 🍪

If you want to add some depth to make some of the shapes more 3D (three-dimensional) then place them on a teaspoon or in the cardboard tube from a kitchen roll that has been cut in half and lined with greaseproof paper. You can also buy foam pads that have grooves in them.

Once your decorations have dried for a few hours you can use them to decorate your cakes and cupcakes or store them in an airtight container until you need them. They will keep well for a month or more, so it's always useful to make up a few extras each time you are cutting out decorations.

🧁 IDEAS FOR DECORATING 🧁 CUPCAKES

There are many, many different ways to make your cupcakes look stunning and when it comes to piping buttercream and choosing the perfect colour combinations, practice really does make perfect. There are hundreds of books and ideas on the internet to give you inspiration and gradually, after trying a few techniques out, you'll begin to develop your own style.

You don't need to rush out and buy a whole set of nozzles and piping bags; chances are the majority would stay sitting, untouched, in your kitchen drawer. All you need to begin with is a large star nozzle (such as a Wilton 1M), a smaller star shaped nozzle, a grass-tip nozzle (great for piping grass or fur on animal cupcakes) and a small round nozzle for piping writing.

Pocket tip 🧍

Practise piping your designs on sheets of greaseproof paper until you get the action and pressure correct. Draw some circles the size of cupcake tops to give you a guideline.

PIPING SWIRLS

One of the most popular piping techniques is to pipe large swirls of buttercream piled up on the top. For this you will need a large star nozzle, such as the Wilton 1M.

1. Fit your nozzle and fill the bag with buttercream.

2. Stand so you are directly above the cupcake and starting from the outside working inwards, apply an even pressure and begin

to move in decreasing circles so the buttercream slightly over-laps itself as you move towards the centre.

3. To finish your swirl, stop applying the pressure and lift the nozzle in a fairly sharp motion upwards away from the cake.

4. Add your sprinkles or sugar paste decorations.

Pocket tip 🍪

If you find it hard to apply the pressure to get the icing to come out, maybe you need to loosen it with a splash more milk.

PIPING ROSE SWIRLS

These are the pretty swirls that resemble roses and sit flatter on the surface of the cupcake.

1. Fit your piping bag with a large star tip nozzle and fill with buttercream.

2. This time you will be starting from the inside and working outwards.

3. Stand directly over the cupcake with your nozzle pointing at the centre. Apply an even pressure and work outwards in increasing sized circles.

4. To finish, stop applying pressure and gently touch the butter-cream against the swirl to hide the end.

Pocket tip 🍪

If you find it hard to hide the end of the buttercream swirl to begin with, place a little sugar paste flower to hide it.

DIPPING CUPCAKES

You can make colourful tops to your cupcakes by dipping them in hundreds and thousands, silver balls or coloured chocolate beans.

- Use a small palette knife to smooth some buttercream over the top of your cupcake.

- Place the sprinkles in a shallow bowl or saucer.

- Turn the cupcake upside down and dip the top into the sprinkles, making sure they coat the top all over.

- Add a piped swirl and sugar paste decoration to finish.

SHOP-BOUGHT DECORATIONS

Supermarkets have greatly increased their cake decorating ranges recently and you can get lots of interesting decorations to try out. For example:

- Orange and lemon jelly slices are the perfect decoration for lemon and poppy seed cupcakes.

- Angelica and pretty sugar roses can be presented on the top of a cupcake to look like a bouquet of flowers.

- Chocolate stars look great stuck into large swirls of dark or white chocolate buttercream.

- Disney and television character decorations can be used by children in their baking.

You can also get the good old traditional decorations that are always handy to keep in your cupboard, such as hundreds and thousands, chocolate sprinkles, jelly diamonds and silver balls.

In cake shops you can get slightly more specialised decorations such as edible glitter and lustre dust, and you can also buy ready-made sugar flowers and hand-crafted cake toppers.

Applying edible glitter

It's quite tricky to apply just the right amount of glitter without it looking too over the top. The best way to do it is to dip the tip of a teaspoon into the glitter then gently tap the top of the handle to sprinkle the glitter over the cupcake.

🧁 PRESENTATION 🧁

There are so many pretty cake stands and plates on sale nowadays that there is absolutely no excuse not to present your cakes beautifully and make them stand out from the crowd. Even if your budget is limited, there are plenty of presentation ideas that won't break the bank. Use your imagination and let your creativity run wild, after all, a well-presented cake is much more appealing than one just plonked on an old plate!

If you are presenting your cake on a cake drum then put some matching ribbon around the edge and fix it with some double-sided tape or edible glue. A large cake looks great on a pedestal cake stand, which creates some height and acts as a lovely centrepiece for your party table.

When serving cakes and scones for afternoon tea, cut your cakes into smaller portions and present them on multi-tiered cake stands or plates decorated with doilies. Cupcakes look great not only when presented in this way but also on glass cake stands with domed lids and in tall cupcake towers. You can even buy disposable cardboard cupcake stands that are decorated in pretty colours, which are fantastic for children's birthday parties.

CUPCAKE STANDS FOR CAKE BUSINESSES

If you are thinking of running your own cake decorating business it's highly likely that you will be asked to create tall towers of cupcakes for weddings and parties, and nine times out of 10 the client will want to hire a stand from you. It is a very good idea to invest in at least two good quality, sturdy stands – one round and one square.

You may also want to consider:

- Charging a refundable deposit to make sure that if your stand isn't returned or is damaged, you have funds to replace it.

- Charging a small amount for hiring out the stand – don't forget that over time it will become scratched or rickety and will need replacing.

- Agreeing on a time and place where you will collect the stand from after the event or asking for it to be returned to you by a certain date.

- Setting out all your hire charges and terms and conditions in a document and making sure whoever is hiring the stand from you signs it to say they are in agreement with your terms.

Cupcakes for special occasions

- *Valentine's Day*. Red velvet cupcakes are the perfect cupcake for Valentine's Day because of their deep red colour. Decorate them with big swirls of cream cheese frosting and red sugar paste hearts.
- *Easter*. To create the perfect cupcakes for Easter use a chocolate cupcake recipe. Spread the tops of the cupcakes with chocolate buttercream, top with flaked chocolate to make a nest shape and add coloured chocolate mini-eggs.
- *Weddings*. For simple but effective wedding cupcakes use a delicious vanilla cupcake recipe. Spread a layer of vanilla buttercream on the top then arrange silver balls into two interlocking ring shapes. Use a tiny sugar paste flower to add detail to one of the rings.
- *Children's birthday parties*. Children love colourful cupcakes so sprinkles are ideal. Spread vanilla cupcakes with buttercream then dip the tops in colourful hundreds and thousands. Add a small buttercream swirl and sugar paste decoration.
- *Fourth of July*. For those who like to celebrate Independence Day spread your favourite cupcake with blue buttercream. Add a white buttercream swirl and top with a red star. Add a sprinkle of gold edible glitter for some sparkle.

BAKING SOLUTIONS

Don't worry, we've all been there! Sometimes things just don't quite go to plan – the cake doesn't rise, the pastry is burnt or the cupcakes have risen too much! There is almost always something that can be done to remedy the situation and if not, find out why it happened so you don't repeat your mistake.

Here are some of the most common problems in baking and some suggestions as to what went wrong and how to put it right.

🧁 THE CAKE DIDN'T RISE 🧁

Usually if your cake didn't rise, it's because you didn't have enough raising agent, such as baking powder, or you used too much liquid in the recipe.

- If you are making a sponge cake, try using an extra teaspoon of baking powder in the mixture.

- If your raising agent was the air in the whisked eggs, you probably didn't whisk them for long enough. Next time make sure they have greatly increased in volume and have become pale in colour. Always fold flour in with a large metal spoon and don't over mix or you will knock the air out.

- If the cake has turned out soggy, it's likely you used too much liquid in your recipe. Try leaving a few tablespoons of the water or milk out of the recipe.

- Make sure you don't open your oven door too soon into the baking process. The rush of cold air can stop the raising agent and can even cause the cake to sink instead of rise.

Cover your tracks

Nine times out of 10, even of your cake didn't rise very well, it will still taste fine. Try serving it with some custard or cover it up with a thick layer of buttercream or whipped cream.

🧁 THE CAKE ROSE TOO MUCH 🧁

The most likely cause for this happening is that you used too much raising agent, your oven was on too high a heat or you put too much mixture into the tin or cake cases.

- Try turning your oven to a lower temperature than the recipe suggests. Ovens vary greatly and you have to experiment to find out what works for your oven. Sometimes if it is too hot your cakes and cupcakes can rise to a peak in the centre.

- Use less raising agent than the recipe suggests – try taking out $1/2$tsp from the recipe next time you bake it.

- Don't overfill your cake tin or cupcake cases. To get nice flat tops to your cupcakes you only need to fill the cake cases half to two-thirds full; any more and you risk them rising too much.

- If your cake mixture has run over the sides of the tin, it's likely your tin was too small. Try the next size up when you bake the recipe again, or bake it in two smaller tins.

Cover your tracks

The best thing to do if your cake rises too much is to level the surface with a sharp knife before decorating it. You can easily cut the peaks off the top of cupcakes and no-one will be any the wiser once you have decorated them with buttercream and pretty sprinkles.

You can also trim the peak off a larger cake then flip it over so the top becomes the bottom and vice versa, giving your cake a nice flat top after all.

🧁 THE PASTRY BURNT 🧁

If you've burnt your pastry it's probably because you had your oven too hot, or left the pastry in there too long.

- Try turning the temperature of your oven down. Remember, all ovens vary and the temperature in the recipe is just a guideline.

- Try baking the pastry on a lower shelf in the oven. The oven will be hotter at the top than at the bottom.

- Keep an eye on the pastry during the baking process – maybe it doesn't need to bake for as long in your oven as the recipe states.

Cover your tracks

Sometimes you can easily just cut the burnt bits off and serve it up with some extra custard or cream. If it is burnt beyond repair, try scooping the filling out and serving it in a different way, for example with custard or make it into part of an ice cream sundae.

THE FRUIT SANK TO THE BOTTOM

This can often happen when baking with dried fruit and in particular, glacé cherries.

- It's always best to coat the dried fruit in some flour before adding it to the recipe and this usually stops it from sinking to the bottom of your cake.

- Maybe the pieces of dried fruit are too large. If you chopped them yourself, try chopping them smaller next time.

- It's always best to wash dried fruit, including those coated with sugar syrup, thoroughly. Leaving the syrup on can make them heavy and slippery so they can sink to the bottom.

Cover your tracks

Usually, the cake will still taste great even if the fruit has sunk to the bottom; it may not look quite as impressive though. Try serving it up with confidence and ignore the appearance or cut it up into small pieces, putting to one side the bits with no fruit in, and serve it on a pretty plate.

🧁 IT'S STUCK TO THE TIN 🧁

It can be so upsetting when you've spent ages making a cake, it comes out from the oven looking and smelling beautiful, but it steadfastly refuses to leave the tin!

- Try running a palette knife around the edge of the cake to see if you can loosen it. Sometimes a little gentle persuasion can work wonders!

- Make sure you always line the tin with greaseproof paper or baking parchment, or grease the tin well if you can't use lining paper.

- Invest in some springform or loose bottom baking tins – it's much easier to release stubborn cakes from these types of tin.

Cover your tracks

Sometimes you can get the cake out with minor damage and a few bits missing can easily be covered with some icing or a sweet sauce. It might be possible to cut it into slices and just serve the pieces that aren't broken too badly.

If all else fails get it out of the tin in any way you can and use the cake crumbs to make something else! Cake balls are becoming very popular now. Crumble the cake, mix with a couple of teaspoons of buttercream until you can form it into small balls, chill for an hour then cover with melted chocolate. No-one will ever know that the cake had gone wrong!

🧁 THE CAKE IS TOO DRY 🧁

Sometimes the lovely moist cake that you were hoping for turns out rather dry and disappointing. It may be that you left it in the oven too long or that you didn't add enough liquid.

- Check the baking times and oven temperature recommendation in the recipe. Perhaps you left it in too long or had the oven too high – or both! Try baking on a lower heat setting next time and keep an eye on the cake near to the end of the baking time. If it's browning too fast, cover the top with some baking parchment or foil.

- Perhaps there wasn't enough liquid in your recipe. Try adding a couple of tablespoons of milk to the cake batter before baking, or perhaps you didn't add enough eggs, so try one more.

Cover your tracks

If your cake has turned out too dry you may be able to save it by moistening it with some sugar syrup. Place 75g caster or granulated sugar and 75ml water into a small saucepan and bring to the boil. Remove from the heat and allow to cool before spreading over the cakes with a pastry brush. You can also add flavourings such as 1tsp vanilla extract or 1tbsp limoncello liqueur.

You can also liven up some dry cake with buttercream. Split the cake, fill it with buttercream and jam then spread more buttercream over the top and round the sides.

🧁 THE ICING IS TOO RUNNY 🧁

With most types of icing the simple answer is that you probably haven't added enough icing sugar.

- If you are making a glacé icing, just stir in extra icing sugar, a tablespoon at a time until you get the consistency you want.

- With buttercream, it may be that your butter was too soft to begin with. Whilst the butter needs to be softened, if it is too runny then it is difficult to work with. Add extra icing sugar, a tablespoon at a time until it firms up.

Cover your tracks

This one is usually fairly easy to save, just by adding more icing sugar to the recipe. However, if you run out of icing sugar you might be able to get away with using the thin icing just as a glaze. Try flavouring it with some lemon or orange juice or adding some cocoa powder, before pouring it over the cake.

🧁 THE BREAD DIDN'T RISE 🧁

Bread baking is a bit of an exact science, a bit too much or not enough of one ingredient can have an effect on how the yeast reacts.

The same goes for temperature, too hot or too cold then the yeast may not be activated.

- Did you actually add the yeast? It's easy to miss out an ingredient by mistake and the bread won't rise without it! Also check the expiry date as old yeast will become inactive.

- Check you added enough yeast, maybe you need to add a little bit more to the recipe.

- Bread needs strong bread flour, which has a higher gluten content than plain flour. Check you used the right flour in your loaf.

- Make sure the liquid you added to the recipe was lukewarm. If it is too hot or too cold, it can kill the yeast or not activate it.

- Make sure you didn't add too much salt and sugar. A little sugar is good to help the yeast work but too much can slow it down, meaning the bread rises less.

Cover your tracks

Unfortunately, this can be a tricky one to cover up. If your bread doesn't rise it will be dense and tough. You might be able to get away with using it in a bread pudding, by soaking the bread in water.

🧁 THE MIXTURE HAS CURDLED 🧁

This doesn't necessarily mean that something has gone wrong and it's often easy to save the recipe in most situations.

- Often when you are making a cake and you have to add the eggs to the fat and sugar, the mixture will look as if it is starting to curdle. Simply add a tablespoon of flour each time you add some egg to your batter and this will prevent it from curdling.

- If you are heating butter and adding ingredients, the mixture may start to split. A brisk whisk is often enough to bring it back together but in the worst cases, sometimes you can pour the excess butter off and carry on.

Cover your tracks

If you can't save the mixture by trying the options above, it may be difficult to cover this one up! If you think your cake mix looks curdled before it goes into the oven then try baking it anyway – often it will come out fine. If your sauce has split or is lumpy try passing it through a sieve before serving it.

🧁 I DON'T HAVE A PARTICULAR 🧁 INGREDIENT

Often it is easy to substitute one ingredient for another, unless you are missing an important main ingredient. Here are some common substitutions that will work well.

- If you don't have any self-raising flour use plain flour instead but add a teaspoon of baking powder and $\frac{1}{2}$tsp salt for every 200g of flour that you use.

- To make a simple substitute for 1tsp baking powder use $\frac{1}{4}$tsp bicarbonate of soda and $\frac{1}{4}$tsp cream of tartar.

- Buttermilk can sometimes be tricky to find in the shops but you can make an easy substitute yourself. Put 1tbsp of lemon juice or white vinegar into a measuring jug then top up with milk to the 250ml mark. Give it a stir and leave for 5 minutes before using.

- If you run out of eggs you can often get away with substituting them with milk. Just add 250ml milk for every egg you would have used. You can also use mayonnaise as a substitute for eggs in cakes – use 3tbsp per egg.

🧁 I DON'T HAVE THAT PIECE OF 🧁 EQUIPMENT

If you don't have a piece of equipment that is stated in the recipe you can often get round it by using something else.

- Whilst it may make life easier, you don't need electrical equipment to help you mix up a recipe. Rubbing in can be done using your fingers instead of a food processor, you can use a wooden spoon to beat the mixture and bread can be kneaded by hand and baked in the oven instead of in a bread machine.

- If you don't have the right size of cake tin that you need use a different shape or size. If you need a deep cake tin and you don't have one, use two shallow tins and sandwich the cake together with some jam or buttercream.

- Look for items that are similar to the equipment that you are missing, for example, if you can't find a whisk to beat the egg with, use a fork.

Pocket fact ▬

A nine tier wedding cake worth $1.3 million (approximately £900,000) and covered in 1,200 carats of diamonds claimed the title of most expensive wedding cake when it was unveiled in Dallas, Texas in 2010.